The New Advertising

Robert Glatzer

THE NEW ADVERTISING

The Great Campaigns From Avis to Volkswagen

The Citadel Press, New York

First Edition
Copyright © 1970 by Robert Glatzer
All rights reserved
Published by Citadel Press, Inc.
A subsidiary of Lyle Stuart, Inc.
222 Park Avenue South
New York, N.Y. 10003
In Canada: George J. McLeod Limited
73 Bathurst Street, Toronto 2B, Ontario
Designed by Reeva Starkman
Printed by Sowers Printing Company
Manufactured in the United States of America
Library of Congress catalog card number: 72-111696
ISBN 0-8065-0009-3

To Newt, for getting me into the business;
and to Paula, for getting me out.

Contents

Introduction

Once upon a time, in the bad old days, the president of Procter & Gamble came to New York from his headquarters in Cincinnati to pay a visit to his advertising agencies. He stopped first at 347 Madison Avenue, headquarters of Dancer-Fitzgerald-Sample, where he indirectly controlled the careers of 112 people working to promote Oxydol, Dreft and Thrill detergents—all Procter & Gamble products. He told them he was not very satisfied with their work.

Then he walked down the street to 285 Madison Avenue to visit Young & Rubicam, where he met sixty-three people devoting their lives to advertising Cheer—another Procter & Gamble detergent. He told them he was not very satisfied with *their* work either.

That afternoon, he stopped in at Grey Advertising, over on Third Avenue, where he listened to reports on Top Job, Joy and Duz—all of them P&G detergents. Joy was outselling Thrill, but Dreft was beating Duz. He said he was pleased with Joy, but unhappy about the others.

Back on Madison Avenue, he visited Compton Advertising, where 217 people worked on P&G's Dash, Tide and Ivory Liquid detergents. He learned that Tide was beating Oxydol, but that Cheer was outselling Dash, Tide and Ivory Liquid. He told Compton that he might have to take the account away and give it to Young & Rubicam.

Early the next morning, he caught the company jet to Chicago, where he dropped in on Tatham-Laird & Kudner, to check up on Bold and Mr. Clean. He was told that Mr. Clean was holding his own, but that Bold was losing out to Dash, though still ahead of Cheer, Tide, Oxydol, Joy and Duz. He told them to dig in and get creative, or else.

The next day he went home to Cincinnati, gave the Thrill account to Compton, the Tide account to Grey, the Top Job and Bold accounts to Young & Rubicam, and the Dreft account to Tatham-Laird. Then he rested from his labors.

Ninety-four people were fired as the result of his trip, not counting media buyers and secretaries, and sixty-one were hired from other agencies to bring new "creative" blood to the accounts. Most of the ninety-four found jobs sooner or later at other agencies, but a few gave up entirely, retiring as "failures" from the business.

Though the story is apocryphal, it points up some of the inanities of the advertising business, where essentially identical products, made by the same company and sold in the same markets, are promoted against each other in the fiercest possible competition—and where thousands of people devote their entire working lives to the struggle. A list of these products

—in addition to detergents—would include cosmetics, patent medicines, beers, cooking oils, company images, soft drinks, airlines and, of course, cigarettes, a rapidly disappearing advertising item.

But it is this identity of product that has, ironically, made it possible for advertising to become so much better than it used to be. For many product categories, these days, the *only* difference between competing brands is the advertising. Now, for the first time in the advertising business, a premium is being placed on imagination. Today's advertising man (or woman) considers himself a professional hired for his talent, not his enthusiasm. His work is much franker and less pretentious than it used to be.

Not that there is a conspiracy against the client. No one is out—yet—to kill the product he works on. But it used to be that agency people were regarded as parasites, hangers-on to the *real* creators, the production and sales people. Today, with markets so large that no sales force could possibly cover them adequately, the agencies have come into their own. Copywriters and art directors have fewer taboos, smarter company advertising managers, and smaller client logotypes to contend with when they make their commercials or print ads. The advertising budget, originally conceived as a tax deduction, is now put to good use. Clients want the *best* (i.e., most "creative") agency, rather than the one with the biggest research or marketing department. It is this change in emphasis that *The New Advertising* is really about: the growth of "creativity" in the advertising business, with creativity defined as a combination of imagination and taste.

We need not rush to lionize the new ad man; successful, imaginative campaigns can also be morally reprehensible, and one of them is reproduced in this book. Nonetheless, if we are to analyze the campaigns with any objectivity, we must take them on their own terms. Do they reach the audience they aim for? Do they affect that audience? And do they persuade it? Those are the first questions. The morality comes later.

The beginning of the so-called new advertising can be dated quite precisely. In 1949, two extremely talented advertising men founded their own agencies and began making ads based on a respect for their audiences and a respect for their own talents, two attitudes that had been notably lacking prior to that date. In that year, David Ogilvy formed Hewitt, Ogilvy, Benson & Mather (now Ogilvy & Mather), and William Bernbach founded Doyle Dane Bernbach. Realizing that a good advertisement must have some intrinsic value, some virtue, of its own, they maintained that if an advertisement served as nothing more than a flack for the product, puffing it up rather than dealing with it, it would never be good at selling that product. "Treat the consumer as if she

were your wife," said Ogilvy, "because she is. Don't talk down to her."
If what Ogilvy and Bernbach did could be put in one sentence, it would
be that they removed the exclamation point from advertising.

This book is a compilation of some of the most famous campaigns created since 1949, which seem to me to use the skills and styles developed during this period. It begins with the work of Bernbach and Ogilvy, and then picks and chooses among those who have followed them. I have made no attempt to be comprehensive, and there are many gross omissions. A number of campaigns I greatly admire are not included, for reasons of space or repetition of subject matter: J. Walter Thompson's campaign for Pan American World Airways; Young & Rubicam's for Eastern Airlines, Jello, Johnson & Johnson, and the Peace Corps; Batten, Barton, Durstine & Osborne's (and others') for Famous Artists and Writers Schools; Jack Tinker & Partners' for Alka-Seltzer; and Doyle Dane Bernbach for its first Rheingold Beer campaign. Others, perhaps more important to a sociologist, are omitted because the advertising was not, in my opinion, the crucial factor in the story. The first one that comes to mind is Carson/Roberts' campaign for Barbie dolls, a product that could be said to encapsulate the tastes and values of the United States in the mid-twentieth century.

I am immensely grateful to the many people who have discussed with me their roles in the campaigns reproduced here, rehashing at great length what must have been very old stuff indeed. In addition to those mentioned in the body of the book, I would particularly like to thank Jean Boutiette, the Earl of Dunmore, Jack Jones, Neil MacMillan, Gerald and Irene Mayer, Alan Mooney, Cy Schneider and Michael Taylor. Much of the research was done at the library of *Advertising Age*, which kindly made available its files during the two years this book was in preparation. Victor Navasky was merciless in keeping my nose to the grindstone, Lili Partridge gathered all the loose ends, and my wife Paula served as unpaid gadfly-provocateur-copy editor.

1

The Best Agency

WHAT MAKES A GOOD advertising agency is not, as it happens, the success of its clients' products. There are simply too many variables outside the control of the agency—advertising budgets, marketing and sales policies, competitive situations, manufacturing and distribution problems, occasionally even the quality of the product—to use product sales as the crucial test. Instead, what makes a good agency is, very simply, the quality of its advertisements, as judged by a consensus of those who happen to care about such things.

By that standard, it would be hard to deny that Doyle Dane Bernbach is the best advertising agency in the United States. It created the advertising for Volkswagen, Polaroid, Avis Rent A Car, the Jamaica Tourist Office, Ohrbach's department stores, Colombian Coffee (Juan Valdez), Sony television, and many other famous campaigns. Its standard of work is consistently higher than that of any other agency, large or small, and its work has been the greatest single influence on advertising in this country since World War II. Client requests—at other agencies—for "a Doyle Dane Bernbach ad" have become a joke in the business. One advertising commentator, the head of a rival agency, wrote that "Doyle Dane Bernbach, in fact, is a major sociological force today. It has persuaded millions of people to act, and its economic influence on the American scene can only be measured in the billions of dollars. There never was such a 'tastemaker' in the history of this country."

Doyle Dane Bernbach is not the largest agency by far, billing only about half as much annually as J. Walter Thompson Co. (largest in the world), but this is at least partly because many advertisers still think of advertising as a cheap substitute for salesmen, to be used for pushing special price deals (Detroit cars), claiming more than the competition (detergents), or cataloguing the merchandise (department stores); and most agencies give clients what they want. Doyle Dane Bernbach, however, has generally insisted on giving its clients what *it* wants them to run, and has often resigned accounts that will not go along with its ads.

In conducting its business this way, the agency has educated its clients first to accept, and then to demand, better advertising; and it has encouraged other agencies to do work of imagination and taste, thus educating *their* clients in turn. This can be seen in the work of Jack Tinker & Partners (Alka-Seltzer); Wells, Rich, Greene (Benson & Hedges); Papert, Koenig, Lois (Xerox); and Carl Ally (Volvo, Hertz); among others. With the exception of Mr. Ally, at least one present owner of each agency had been hired by William Bernbach as a copywriter or art director within the past ten years.

An interesting little chart can be made up to show the propagation of the faith:

DOYLE DANE BERNBACH
Julian Koenig
George Lois
Mary Wells

PAPERT, KOENIG, LOIS
Julian Koenig
George Lois
Carl Ally

JACK TINKER & PARTNERS
Mary Wells
Richard Rich
Stewart Greene

CARL ALLY INC.
Carl Ally

WELLS, RICH, GREENE
Mary Wells
Richard Rich
Stewart Greene

These people were talented, they learned a great deal from Bernbach, and then they were independent enough to leave him and go out on their own. They built on what he and David Ogilvy started (separately) in 1949, and they have taken advertising to the point where it now dominates, for good or evil, the commercial media that carry it.

But what is it that made Doyle Dane Bernbach so good? Is there a Doyle, a Dane, or a Bernbach and, if so, what do they do all day at the agency?

Well, there is, or are, a Doyle, a Dane, and a Bernbach. Until his retirement in late 1969 Ned Doyle concerned himself with supervising account executives, acting as go-between and interpreter to clients, writers and art directors; encouraging clients to accept the agency's work; and making sure that those who created the advertisements were aware of the business realities involved. Maxwell Dane has been the inside organizer, the financial man, the one who planned and executed the public sale of Doyle Dane Bernbach's stock—the first time a major agency had gone public—and made millionaires of the partners and of some smart outside investors. William Bernbach is just responsible for the advertising.

The three men formed the agency in 1949, when Bernbach and Doyle were both at Grey Advertising and Dane had a small agency of his own. They started with a few of Dane's clients, and brought the Ohrbach's account with them from Grey. By 1969 the agency's United States billings were in excess of $260 million. No other agency had ever grown that fast (Wells, Rich, Greene may soon overtake it: by its fourth birthday, in May of 1969, it had grown from $8 million in billings to $85 million per year).

As to why the agency is so good, the answer is Bernbach. Immensely talented himself, he has also been able to get and hold other talented people, and some of them have turned down enormous offers from other agencies in order to stay with him. "He is brilliant," says Phyllis Robinson, his copy chief since 1949, "he is an extremely hard worker, he has extremely high standards for himself and everyone else, and he is a tremendously enthusiastic person. He is constantly promoting the agency within the agency. It's almost a joke here that when you see him at the water cooler he's always got some news flash about some great thing that we did."

Helmut Krone, the Doyle Dane Bernbach art director who created the Volkswagen and Avis campaigns and invented the character Juan Valdez, says: "In the thirties, if you didn't work for Frank Lloyd Wright, you weren't an architect. Well, we were working for Frank Lloyd Wright. Bill was like a father to me in the early days. Every Monday morning we invented something around here—it was like the Bauhaus. I'll give you an example: Bill came in one day and said, 'How about we make a black page, a whole black page in *The New York Times,* and make a window shade out of it, and we'll say, "Too bad you can't be seen in lingerie from Ohrbach's."'"

"Bernbach has an absolutely childlike enthusiasm for something great," says Robert Gage, whom Bernbach brought over from Grey in 1949 and who has now taken Bernbach's place as creative director of the agency. "He's just in seventh heaven. This isn't a place where you're *free* to create great stuff; it's *demanded* of you. You *have* to create here."

Bernbach's enthusiasm for creative, intuitive work is matched only by his distrust of research, a tool heavily used at most large agencies. "Research has created a lot of advertising technicians who know all the rules. They can tell you that babies and dogs will attract more readers. They can tell you that body copy should be broken up for easier reading. They can tell you all the right things, and give you fact after fact. They're the scientists of advertising. But there's one rub: advertising is fundamentally persuasion, and persuasion happens to be not a science but an art. It is simply not enough to say the right thing. Things have to be said that motivate people. The difference is the art."

Gage adds: "I think there is a great danger in research as a basis to work from. One of the big flops of the century was the . . . what was the name of that car? I don't even recall it now . . . which was an entirely researched design. It had everything everybody wanted, except that nobody wanted it."

"Now, I'm not talking about tricking people," says Bernbach. "If you get attention by a trick, how can people like you for it? For instance, you are not right if, in your ad, you stand a man on his head just to get attention. But you are right if you have him on his head to show how your product keeps things from falling out of his pockets."

Bernbach is saying that "honesty"—an honest appraisal of the client's product, its advantages and sales points, its disadvantages and shortcomings, is essential to good advertising. Insofar as he follows his own dicta, he makes no attempt to disguise product limitations and, in fact, by anticipating objections he hopes that the ad will make its audience feel better about the product's advantages. There is a Volkswagen ad that begins: "If you haven't bought a Volkswagen because you don't like its looks, we can't help you. . . ." Unlike some of his competitors, Bernbach does not sell dreams.

Bernbach runs his creative departments like a father: "After we grew, I deliberately withheld solutions from my people so that they would have the satisfaction of finding the answers themselves. You have to care for your people, let them grow. To look around at other agencies and the work they're doing, and say, 'Who's the best? Let's bring him over here' [he is speaking of Marion Harper, who built the Interpublic agency empire by raiding other agencies for top men], well, he's not the same guy. We've got the depth, and that depth has come by working, by loving, by pleading, by caring." ("He is a genius at letting people be themselves," says Robert Levenson, a copy supervisor who learned his trade under Bernbach.)

Perhaps Bernbach's greatest contribution, even more than his individual campaigns, was his recognition that, to the consumer, advertising is as much a part of a product's makeup as its chemical composition. "Businesses are similar, products are similar. What's left is my ability to make the consumer feel something about my product. *Execution becomes content.* You have to say the right things so that people feel it in the gut. Of course, everybody says, 'I'm the best.' What counts is the artistry with which you say it, so people believe it. Which is not to say that we'll take a poor product; we like to believe in the worth of the product. And anyway, great advertising just makes a bad product fail faster." Bernbach proved this to himself in the summer of 1967, when he did an excellent campaign for a low-carbohydrate beer called Gablinger's, which got hundreds of thousands of New Yorkers to try a can of it. Unfortunately, for most of them one can was more than enough, and by autumn both the beer and the campaign were dead.

The agency operates on a system of teams: one writer and one art director work on each account, or account section, and together they are responsible for all print, television, and radio advertising. The teams are generally assigned by Bernbach or Gage on the basis of matched talent and personality, a tricky procedure in the best of circumstances, but which by and large has worked very well at the agency. There is no veto by account executives, no attenuation of imagination by review committees; what is written is (generally) what runs.

But primarily the system works because of Bernbach. Where David Ogilvy stifled other people's creative work, Bernbach encourages it. Where Julian Koenig and George Lois competed with their employees, Bernbach takes pride in them. Where Leo Burnett shut himself off through a hierarchy of sycophants, Bernbach remains open and available. Even if Bernbach should change, and there are some who think he already has, the system has generated enough momentum to carry it for many more years.

Three of the six Doyle Dane Bernbach campaigns in this book are national campaigns, advertised throughout the country and well known to most people. They are for Polaroid, Avis and Volkswagen. The other three—El Al Israel Airlines, Ohrbach's and Levy's bread—are local or regional campaigns, but have had a great effect on other agencies and on advertising in general, even though they are not well known to the public.

Volkswagen

Or, *The Magic Transformation of the Beetle:
in which a Jewish Advertising Agency turns a Nazi Automobile into the Sixth-Largest-Selling Car in the United States, as William Bernbach, Helmut Krone, and Julian Koenig take a Small, Cheap, Ugly, Slow, Imported German Car, and without laying Hand to Fender change it into a Popular, Desirable, Lovable, Attractive Staple of American Life;*
Or, THANK GOD FOR THE SECOND WORLD WAR; IT BROUGHT US ALL CLOSER TOGETHER.

By 1959 most of West Germany's reparations to Israel and the Jews had been paid, and Americans were feeling rather better about German products. Tens of thousands of Volkswagens were being sold here each year, without a national advertising program, and the company made inquiries as to the best agency to handle the account. They selected Doyle Dane Bernbach; and Krone, who some say looks like a Nazi but who acts like a Jew, and Koenig, who looks like a Jew but is often said to act like a Nazi, were assigned to the account.

The gang trooped off to the Fatherland to watch the cars being built. What could you say about them? It was the Year of the Edsel, and Americans were in love with chrome, streamlining, annual model changes, horsepower— all the necessities of the Age of Eisenhower. To advertise a car with no frills, no glamor, no changes, no power was certainly an interesting challenge.

Is Volkswagen contemplating a change?

The answer is yes.

Volkswagen changes continually throughout each year. There have been 80 changes in 1959 alone.

But none of these are changes you merely see. We do not believe in planned obsolescence. We don't change a car for the sake of change. Therefore the doughty little Volkswagen shape will still be the same.

The familiar snub nose will still be intact.

Yet, good as our car is, we are constantly finding ways to make it better. For instance, we have put permanent magnets in the drain plugs. This will keep the oil free of tiny metal particles, since the metal adheres to the magnets.

Our shift, we are told, is the best in the world. But we found a way to make it even smoother. We riveted special steel springs into our clutch plate lining.

The Volkswagen has changed completely over the past eleven years, but not its heart or face.

 VW owners keep their cars year after year, secure in the knowledge that their used VW is worth almost as much as a new one.

Plate 1

© 1960 VOLKSWAGEN

Lemon.

This Volkswagen missed the boat.

The chrome strip on the glove compartment is blemished and must be replaced. Chances are you wouldn't have noticed it; Inspector Kurt Kroner did.

There are 3,389 men at our Wolfsburg factory with only one job: to inspect Volkswagens at each stage of production. (3000 Volkswagens are produced daily; there are more inspectors than cars.)

Every shock absorber is tested (spot checking won't do), every windshield is scanned. VWs have been rejected for surface scratches barely visible to the eye.

Final inspection is really something! VW inspectors run each car off the line onto the Funktionsprüfstand (car test stand), tote up 189 check points, gun ahead to the automatic brake stand, and say "no" to one VW out of fifty.

This preoccupation with detail means the VW lasts longer and requires less maintenance, by and large, than other cars. (It also means a used VW depreciates less than any other car.)

We pluck the lemons; you get the plums.

Plate 2

Although Krone owned a VW at the time ("That's why I was put on the account"), he says that he seriously misjudged the advertising approach. "I thought we should shoot Suzy Parker next to the car, make it a white man's car. I felt the best thing you could do was talk with a midwestern

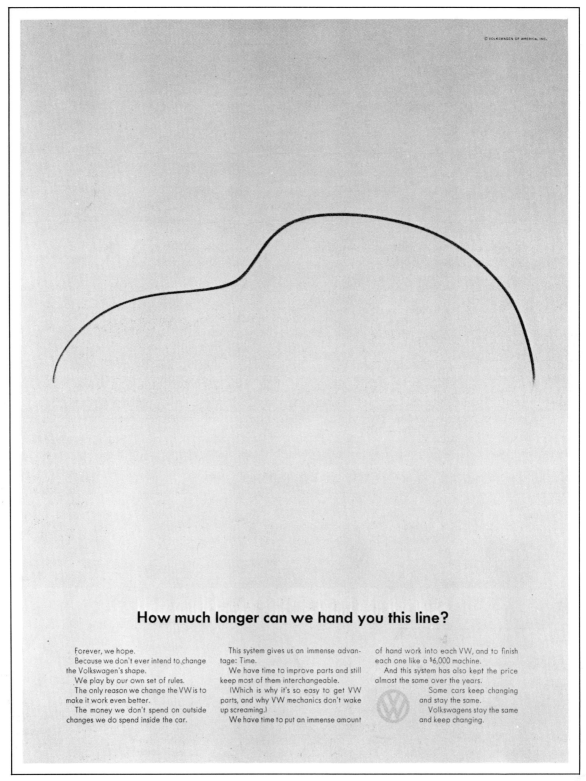

How much longer can we hand you this line?

Forever, we hope.

Because we don't ever intend to change the Volkswagen's shape.

We play by our own set of rules.

The only reason we change the VW is to make it work even better.

The money we don't spend on outside changes we do spend inside the car.

This system gives us an immense advantage: Time.

We have time to improve parts and still keep most of them interchangeable.

(Which is why it's so easy to get VW parts, and why VW mechanics don't wake up screaming.)

We have time to put an immense amount of hand work into each VW, and to finish each one like a $6,000 machine.

And this system has also kept the price almost the same over the years.

Some cars keep changing and stay the same.

Volkswagens stay the same and keep changing.

Plate 3

Plate 4

That's a load off our front.

Now you know why the Volkswagen Station Wagon has that sawed-off look.

There is no front in front because we put our engine in back.

The advantages are obvious:

The Volkswagen is 4 feet shorter than standard wagons, but only 9 inches longer than the Volkswagen Sedan.

It parks like a little sports car.

Yet inside, you can carry more stuff than any wagon made: 1632 lbs.

Then there are a couple of advantages that aren't so obvious.

The VW is nearly a ton lighter on its tires than standard wagons. So 35,000 miles to a set is not unusual.

And you'll never need water. Or anti-freeze. The engine's air-cooled.

You get the kind of mileage people hope for in compact cars, to say nothing of big wagons. (24 mpg is average.)

And you're still pushing a hood in front? When all that could be behind you?

accent. I was wrong." Bernbach made an intuitive decision to turn the liability of the car's appearance into the virtue of honesty. The only way, he felt, to sell the VW in America was as an "honest" car. It had already, in fact, made enough of an impact in Detroit to stir defensive rumblings about building "compact" cars, and the first Ramblers, Corvairs and

Falcons were soon to appear. Bernbach, Krone and Koenig looked for a way to project "honesty" in an imaginative, persuasive fashion, and came up with "Is Volkswagen contemplating a change?" *(Plate 1).*

Bernbach later commented: "People thought of Volkswagen as never

24

©1960 VOLKSWAGEN

Think small.

Ten years ago, the first Volkswagens were imported into the United States.

These strange little cars with their beetle shapes were almost unknown.

All they had to recommend them was 32 miles to the gallon (regular gas, regular driving), an aluminum air-cooled rear engine that would go 70 mph all day without strain, sensible size for a family and a sensible price-tag too.

Beetles multiply; so do Volkswagens. By 1954,

VW was the best-selling imported car in America. It has held that rank each year since. In 1959, over 150,000 Volkswagens were sold, including 30,000 station wagons and trucks.

Volkswagen's snub nose is now familiar in fifty states of the Union; as American as apple strudel. In fact, your VW may well be made with Pittsburgh steel stamped out on Chicago presses (even the power for the Volkswagen plant is supplied by coal from the U.S.A.).

As any VW owner will tell you, Volkswagen service is excellent and it is everywhere. Parts are plentiful, prices low. (A new fender, for example, is only $21.75.*) No small factor in Volkswagen's success.

Today, in the U.S.A. and 119 other countries, Volkswagens are sold faster than they can be made. Volkswagen has become the world's fifth largest automotive manufacturer by thinking small. More and more people are thinking the same. *Suggested retail price.

Plate 5

changing. They were eager to read of a change, and they weren't disappointed, because they learned that while the outside of the car never changed, countless changes are made where they count, inside the car where you can feel and hear them, not outside where it dates the car and

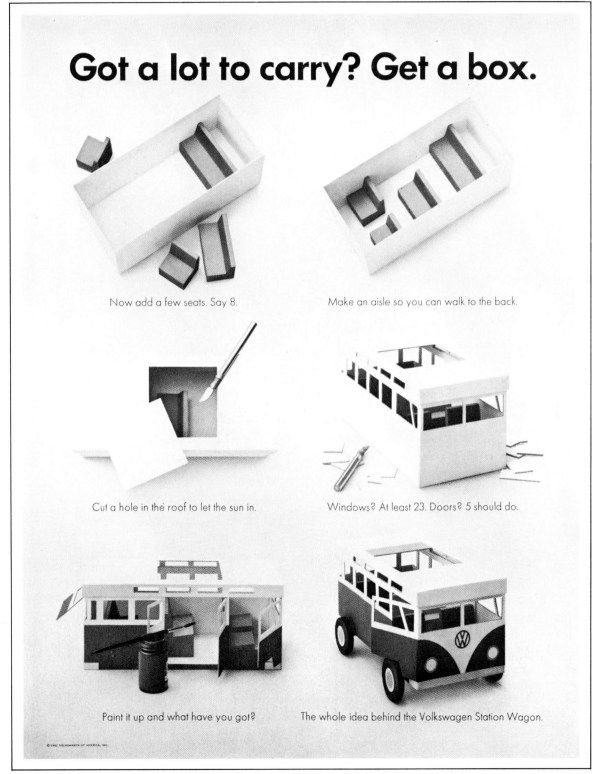

Plate 6

obsoletes it," an attitude which won him the Silk Purse From Sow's Ear Award, Put The Best Face On It Division, for 1959.

With regard to the famous "Lemon" ad *(Plate 2)*, Bernbach said: "This is the classic description for disappointment in a car. Yet here it was used

©1961 BY VOLKSWAGEN OF AMERICA, INC.

Why you should open a window before you close the door of a Volkswagen.

Don't laugh.

Every now and then a new VW owner asks why the doors seem hard to close.

The reason is simple: the Volkswagen is practically airtight.

With the windows up, the door meets a solid wall of trapped air. So it takes a little extra push to close it. (Unless you open a window just a crack to let the air escape.)

It happens because every last VW part fits just so. Which really isn't so surprising: When you've been making the same basic car as long as we have, all the wrinkles get ironed out along the way. For good.

Even so, we still make it a point to inspect every operation all down the line. (We have

3,500 people who do nothing else.)

It's the kind of craftsmanship you may still remember, but not really expect any more.

At the final checkpoint, an inspector cranks up the windows and tries to close a door. Gently.

If it doesn't work, he knows it's perfect.

Plate 7

to prove memorably once again that Volkswagen is an honest car. For it was the ruthless VW inspector who considered this particular car a lemon because it had an almost invisible scratch on the door. Suppose we had merely said, 'Every VW must pass rigid inspections.' How many ads

Regular size.   Large economy size.

Volkswagens come in two handy sizes: Sedan and Station Wagon.

The packages are very different, but the works are about the same.

There is a genuine Volkswagen engine in the back of each. It gives both cars solid traction on ice and snow.

The engines are air-cooled, too. So you never mess with water or anti-freeze.

The VW Sedan seats 4 adults comfortably or 5 adults uncomfortably. (A mother, a father and 3 kids are about right.)

The VW Wagon is only 9 inches longer than the Sedan, a neat trick all by itself.

It seats 8 comfortably, 9 uncomfortably and 10 very uncomfortably, but it's been done. (The kids that fit are countless.)

The VW Sedan averages 32 miles to the gallon, the Wagon a mere 24.

Once upon a time, people had trouble deciding whether to buy a VW or not.

Now they have trouble deciding which size.

Plate 8

and how much money do you think it would have taken to make the same point that was made in one creative stroke with the one-word headline 'Lemon'"?

Plates 3–8 illustrate some of the more famous ads that have run through

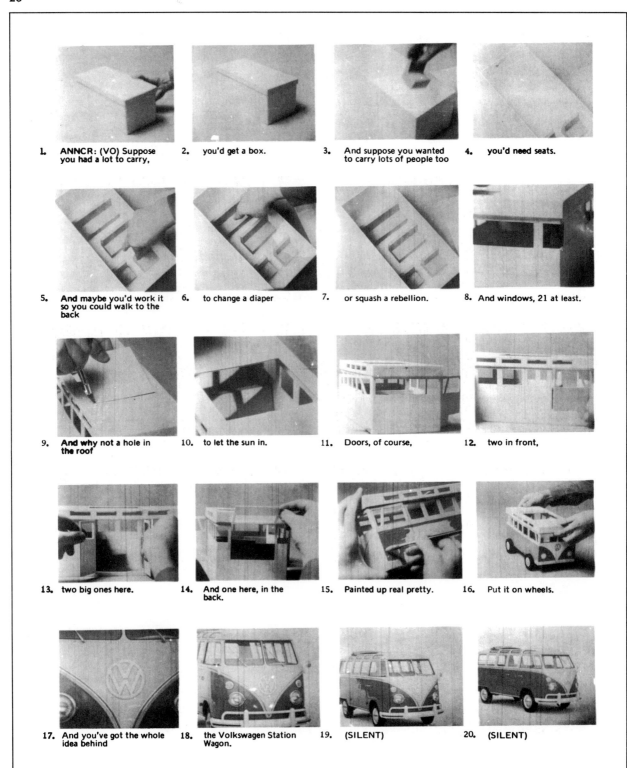

1. ANNCR: (VO) Suppose you had a lot to carry,
2. you'd get a box.
3. And suppose you wanted to carry lots of people too
4. you'd need seats.
5. And maybe you'd work it so you could walk to the back
6. to change a diaper
7. or squash a rebellion.
8. And windows, 21 at least.
9. And why not a hole in the roof
10. to let the sun in.
11. Doors, of course,
12. two in front,
13. two big ones here.
14. And one here, in the back.
15. Painted up real pretty.
16. Put it on wheels.
17. And you've got the whole idea behind
18. the Volkswagen Station Wagon.
19. (SILENT)
20. (SILENT)

Plate 9

Plate 10

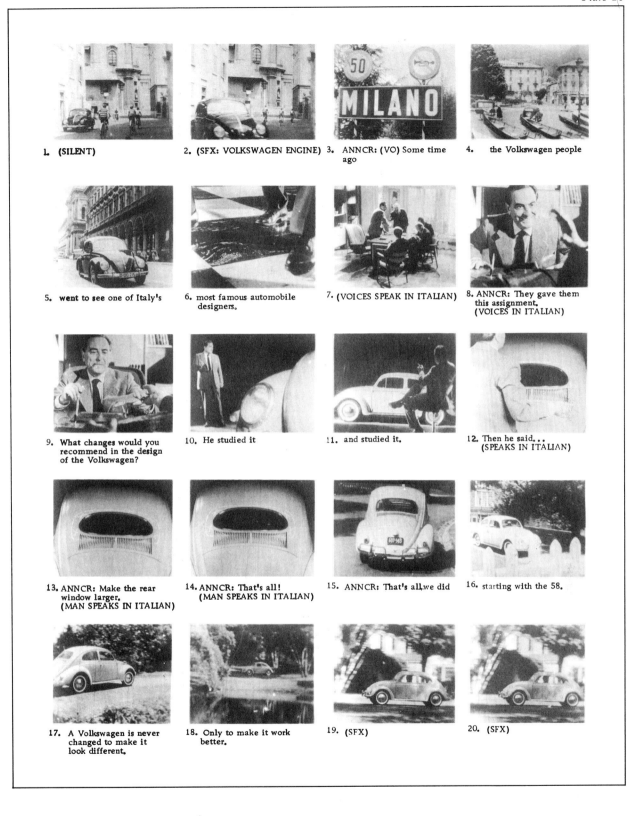

1. (SILENT)

2. (SFX: VOLKSWAGEN ENGINE)

3. ANNCR: (VO) Some time ago

4. the Volkswagen people

5. went to see one of Italy's

6. most famous automobile designers.

7. (VOICES SPEAK IN ITALIAN)

8. ANNCR: They gave them this assignment. (VOICES IN ITALIAN)

9. What changes would you recommend in the design of the Volkswagen?

10. He studied it

11. and studied it.

12. Then he said... (SPEAKS IN ITALIAN)

13. ANNCR: Make the rear window larger. (MAN SPEAKS IN ITALIAN)

14. ANNCR: That's all! (MAN SPEAKS IN ITALIAN)

15. ANNCR: That's all we did

16. starting with the 58.

17. A Volkswagen is never changed to make it look different.

18. Only to make it work better.

19. (SFX)

20. (SFX)

the years. One of Krone's favorite ads was addressed to the automotive trade, and showed a smiling man leaning out of the window of his Rolls-Royce, which is parked in front of a Volkswagen dealership. He is saying, "It's been a good year, here at Volkswagen." The client killed it.

The television commercials have been quite different in style from the print ads, but they have their own consistency of approach and are extremely well done *(Plates 9, 10)*.

Volkswagen has, of course, been a great commercial success in this country, and it is not by any means due entirely to the advertising. The company insisted from the first that VW dealers handle the line exclusively, that they not take on any other brands. This was unique in the imported-car business, but it gave the dealers pride in their product, and forced them to care about satisfying the customer. It is the point on which Renault and Volvo, the two comparable imports, foundered, because their dealers became careless and lackadaisical, and made little effort to sell the cars. There was always another brand to sell, and advertising, after all, could only get the customers into the showroom.

In addition, the Volkswagen was priced right. In 1959 it sold for almost a thousand dollars less than the cheapest American car; even in 1968 the beetle was still three hundred dollars less than the lowest-priced Rambler. Here, too, Volvo overpriced itself in a short-sighted attempt to get rich quick in America.

In 1959 Volkswagen sold 120,000 cars out of a total imported-car figure of 614,000. It was then, as it is today, the largest-selling imported car. But then Detroit introduced its own compacts, and import sales dropped to a low, in 1962, of 340,000. The sales of every foreign car but Volkswagen declined; their dealers resorted to every Detroit-type discount and advertising gimmick. That year, however, VW sold almost 200,000. By 1967 total import sales reached 700,000, and Volkswagen sold 430,000 of them—more than the sales of all other imported cars combined—and more than any American brand except Impala, Mustang and Plymouth.

Through the years the Volkswagen ads have maintained an extraordinary consistency. "There have been ten teams on the account," says Bernbach, "and I defy you to tell me where one team left off and another one started." But the tone was set by Krone and Koenig, however, which counts for a good deal. The ads have remained representations of the theme of "honesty," with simple layouts, a clean, uncluttered look, and a copy style that is factual and straightforward. The ads are as "honest" as the car.

Polaroid

"Everybody says, 'Well, Polaroid. How can you miss? It's a natural for
advertising. All you have to do is show it.' They forget that Batten, Barton,
Durstine & Osborne had the Polaroid account for five years before we
got it, and it looked like shit. In fairness to them, I will say that it was
BBDO's Boston office, but still I think somebody over there might have
recognized what they had." So said one Doyle Dane Bernbach art director.
Plate 11 shows a fairly typical BBDO ad for Polaroid. The reader may
judge for himself.

Plate 11

"When we got the account in 1954," says Phyllis Robinson, "people felt
that the Polaroid was a nice gimmick, but—. We tried to get people over
this idea of the gimmick. We had to show what a great product idea it
was, and do it as simply as possible. So we told the story in one line:
'How to take a picture one minute and see it the next.' That line said
everything." Helmut Krone and William Casey created a similar ad,
divided into quadrants headed *6:01, 6:02, 6:03, 6:04*. In the first
quadrant a man is getting ready to take a Polaroid picture of his family.
In the second, he snaps the picture. In the third, he peels off the
backing, and in the fourth everyone is looking at the completed picture.
There was no body copy in the ad; simply the Polaroid signature in the
corner.

These early ads are good examples of how Bernbach's people could
convey the essence of a product. They are almost shockingly simple, and

FIRST SHOWING OF A NEW POLAROID LAND FILM. This is an enlargement of an actual 60-second picture of Louis Armstrong. It was taken with a new film, just introduced, which is twice as sharp as the previous film.

With this latest development, the Polaroid Land Camera not only gives you pictures in 60 seconds, but pictures of exceptional clarity and brilliance. Polaroid Land Cameras start at $72.75. The new film can be identified by a star on the box.

Plate 12

GRANDMA MOSES: PHOTOGRAPHED WITH A NEW POLAROID LAND FILM. This is an enlargement of an actual 60-second picture. It was taken with a new film, just introduced, which is twice as sharp as the previous film. With this latest advance, the Polaroid Land Camera not only gives you pictures in 60 seconds, but pictures of astonishing quality. Polaroid Land Cameras start at $72.75. The new film can be identified by a star on the box.

Plate 13

by virtue of their own simplicity they convey to the reader that taking pictures with a Polaroid camera must also be simple. To amateurs who for years had taken their exposed film to the drugstore and then waited a week for prints, and to those who had never taken pictures because it seemed so complicated, this was revolutionary.

In 1957 Polaroid introduced a black-and-white film so sensitive that pictures could be taken by the light of one candle—a remarkable innovation to have come from a competitor of Kodak, which had dominated the field for so long. In addition, the new film had a finer grain structure (giving sharpness to the image) and a more even response to light from white down to black (which meant a more accurate rendition of the subject) than did any Kodak film. Krone did a series of ads designed to show off the quality of the film, using photographs taken by the well-known fashion photographer Bert Stern *(Plates, 12, 13)*.

That year, the agency began advertising Polaroid on television, with live commercials on Steve Allen's *Tonight* show. They were perhaps the best advertising demonstrations ever done on television. Since the camera could take and develop pictures in sixty seconds, the standard duration of a commercial, the spots consisted simply of Allen photographing someone on stage with him, pulling the print out to start the developing process, and talking about the camera while the picture was developing. After one minute, he would peel the backing off and show the picture to the audience. It never failed to get a round of applause, and for the same reasons that a good magic act gets it: there is suspense, and then a pleasurable release of tension. The commercials showed that this peculiar camera could take fine pictures, that anyone could take them, and that even under tense, difficult circumstances they would come out well. The commercials ran for four years on the show, by which time enough cameras were out in people's hands to let them make their own commercials.

Beginning in 1961 the Polaroid commercials and advertisements concentrated more on pictures than on the process. Howard Zieff, a photographer known for his ability to capture down-to-earth situations, was hired to shoot a series of ads designed to evoke emotional memories and anticipations that would relate to most American families. They have been the mainstay of Polaroid advertising ever since *(Plates 14–16)*.

To go along with this print campaign, or rather to lead it, Gage and Mrs. Robinson created a series of human-emotion commercials that have run, with refinements, up to the present. Some of them have brought viewers to tears by their portrayal of sentimental, touching moments, which is rather an accomplishment in sixty seconds of commercial time. It is even possible to say that these commercials, on occasion, touch art, for, like art, they have nonlinear communication with their audience, where in the instant of recognition of the situation created in the commercial,

Happiness is contagious. So is the Polaroid Land Camera. Isn't it time your family started taking 10-second pictures?

Plate 14

POLAROID ®

THIS PICTURE came out of a Polaroid Land Camera in ten seconds. It's the kind of picture you have to get while the getting's good; the kind you wouldn't want to lose. If it's a Polaroid Land Camera, you don't lose it. You see the finished picture in ten seconds and you know if you've got it. If not, there's still time to take another one before the picture goes away forever. Pictures like this of your family can be coming out of your Polaroid Land Camera all during the fall, if you get one now. And, by early spring, it will be possible for you to take color pictures out of the same camera.

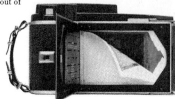

Plate 15

the audience perceives more than one level of meaning. These overtones, like those which distinguish the sound of a flute from that of a Coke bottle, are responsible for the emotion. Advertising essays, the more traditional form, rarely have the power to do that.

Perhaps it is this quality that enabled Doyle Dane Bernbach to make the transition to television advertising so well, back in the mid-1950s. The

Plate 16

agency's writers and art directors, accustomed to communicating images rather than sequences of didactic points, found it unnecessary to load up commercials with blackboard lectures or men in white coats. To this day, many agencies have not successfully made the transition.

One of the most famous Polaroid commercials is called "After the wedding." It is a beautifully photographed film of the father and mother of the bride. They are obviously middle-aged, with lovely, even sad faces. The film begins as they kiss their daughter goodbye and watch her leave with her husband to begin her own life. The sounds of the celebration leave with them, too, and the father and mother turn around to take a last look at the reception room, now quiet and empty. They wander past the messy tables, littered with the remains of the champagne and wedding cake, walking hand in hand, alone now for the rest of their lives. They come to their own table and pick up some Polaroid pictures of the wedding—spontaneous, unposed, informal—recapturing the spirit of the day.

"People say that commercial is so moving," says Mrs. Robinson. "What is it? Well, a lot of it wouldn't be possible if Bob Gage and I couldn't say we're human, and we're touched by things, and we put our feelings on the screen. Not to use the tender feelings between people, not to use people's hopes and cares, is abdicating your responsibility. That commercial is an example of this expression of feeling. We had to have the conviction not only that we could get across the feeling of the wedding, but that we could go beyond the triteness of the situation. We felt it was possible to use the tenderer human emotions in advertising without getting icky; and it's a hell of a selling tool."

Ohrbach's

The Ohrbach's department store campaign is included here because it shows in microcosm the development of the Doyle Dane Bernbach style, from its erratic beginnings in the 1940s at Grey Advertising, to the first consistently imaginative work that began appearing in the 1950s.

Ohrbach's was the first account Doyle Dane Bernbach ever had, coming over with the agency principals from Grey; and, because the store itself is so unique, it might be helpful to discuss it briefly first. Ohrbach's started on 14th Street in New York, in 1923, handling low-end, job-lot quantities of women's clothes. It outgrew its competitors, moved to 34th Street, and opened branches in suburban New York, Newark and Los Angeles. It has gradually become known as one of the fashion leaders for women's

if you are over or under 35*...you need

SNIAGRAB

(spell it backwards)

Do you feel dull and uninteresting? Do you pass by crowds of men and never even hear a whistle? Have you lost that bright look and that quick step? Don't worry! It's really not your age. All you need is SNIAGRAB from Ohrbach's.

Ohrbach's bargains in the very latest suits are "just what the doctor ordered" for giving your spirits a lift. It's a perfect prescription that blends the newest fashion with amazingly low prices. The sooner you take it the sooner you'll feel better.

*if you are exactly 35 . . . happy birthday!

Ohrbach's
NEW YORK • NEWARK • LOS ANGELES

"A BUSINESS IN MILLIONS...A PROFIT IN PENNIES"
NEW YORK: 14th STREET FACING UNION SQUARE • NEWARK: MARKET AND HALSEY STREETS

Plate 17

clothing and accessories in the United States. Among other things, it has become famous for its copies of Paris originals, often putting them on sale within a week of the showings.

Ohrbach's achieved its position by violating every rule of good merchandising known to the trade. It holds no sales, announces no promotions, never shows marked-down values on merchandise (instead of crossing off the old price and writing in the new, as is commonly done in retailing, the store removes the whole price tag and replaces it with another that shows only the new price), and removes all designer labels from clothing. In 1967 Ohrbach's first offered its customers charge accounts, but otherwise all is as it was in 1923: no deliveries, no wrapping service, no C.O.D.s, no mail or phone orders, no alterations. "We are not a discount store," says Mark Klauser, director of advertising and public relations, "though we take only half the markup (20 per cent) of other stores. We are an underselling store, and you can't undersell unless you cut out certain services."

In its advertising, too, Ohrbach's has been unique. It runs only institutional advertisements, and for more than forty years, until 1966, not one had ever so much as mentioned the price of an item. "Our ads stress high fashion and high quality at a low price," says Judy Protas, who has been copywriter on the account since 1951. "We sell the store as a whole, and not just specific items. Everything in the ads converges at one point, which is the presentation of Ohrbach's as the solution to the customer's needs." Finally, Ohrbach's has always been the only major New York department store that does not make its own advertisements, having hired Grey in 1930. Doyle Dane Bernbach got the account because Bernbach, Doyle and Gage all worked on it at Grey—Bernbach as creative director, Gage as art director, and Doyle as account executive.

All of the agency principals look back on their long association with Ohrbach's with great pleasure and affection, recalling many of its ads as their favorites. But of all the famous campaigns that have been done by this group, their early Ohrbach's ads are, surprisingly, the most old-fashioned, overly cute, ineptly photographed and badly laid out. Much of the copy—by itself—is good, sometimes even brilliant (written by Bernbach and by Phyllis Robinson, as well as Miss Protas):

If you are over or under 35* . . . you need SNIAGRAB (spell it backwards) . . . *If you are exactly 35, happy birthday. (1952)

LIBERAL TRADE-IN: Bring in your wife and just a few dollars . . . we will give you a new woman. (1952)

When I saw how low the price was, I thought I'd die. (1957)

The photography and graphic elements are a little more picturesque *(Plates 17–19)*. They were derivative of a style of art direction invented by Paul Rand, who was head of the art department at Grey in the 1940s. It was his contention that an advertisement should work on the reader like a painting. He regarded the entire page or area of the ad as a canvas, whose elements could be placed anywhere within it so long as they contributed to the total effect. He chose type faces for design value rather than for ease of readership, and often broke up copy lines in order to relate them better to the illustration. He freed art directors from the

41

Plate 18

Plate 19

42

tyranny of type faces like **FRANKLIN GOTHIC** and NEWS GOTHIC, whose power had been vitiated by years of overuse and which in any case were more suitable to old-fashioned table-thumping rhetoric than to the conveying of emotion, pleasure or beauty.

Rand, as a theorist, was to have a profound effect on men like Gage and Helmut Krone, and on their followers, the young art directors of the 1960s, enabling them to think of space—or time, in the case of a television commercial—as an entity to be filled in any way appropriate to the subject or theme of the ad. But Rand, as an art director, never had the talent to make great advertisements himself, and Gage's work of the early 1950s shows that he still had not freed himself from imitations of an essentially weak style. It was not until the Polaroid campaign of 1954, in fact, that he began building on Rand's theories instead of his style, and began doing the kind of work that was to make him famous in the business.

Nonetheless, even the early Ohrbach's ads were oases in the bleak desert of retail advertising. They were involving; they had the quality of talking to the reader when most stores simply talked to themselves; they were lively, sometimes funny, and they could be read with pleasure all the way to the bottom of the page. They created an image for the store that made it the quintessence of inexpensive chic for every woman in New York.

Most of all, they provided a training ground in which Bernbach could test his own approach to advertising. Because the store had already broken all the conventions of merchandising and retail advertising, Bernbach did not have to fight the battle again. He was free to improvise on Ohrbach's themes, and to take as a guide for future accounts the ability to forget stereotypes and the phrase "That's the way it's always been done," and look instead for new solutions. Because Ohrbach's theme never changed (high fashion and high quality at low prices was the only message, and it had already been running for fifteen years before Bernbach even came to Grey), and because institutional instead of merchandise and sales ads had been Ohrbach's approach, all Bernbach had to do was keep them going, and look for more imaginative ways of doing it. It is no denigration of Bernbach's talent, or of his own contributions, to point out that he did not conceive the Ohrbach's theme.

Perhaps the most effective single advertisement in retailing came out of this approach. It was done by Bernbach and Gage (*Plate 20*). The ad ran only once, in 1957, though it was later used in subway posters (another Doyle Dane Bernbach idea, perfect for institutional advertising though rarely used by other department stores), and requests for reprints are still coming in.

Bernbach has often said that the Ohrbach's account has been his best salesman. "We have never had a new-business department," he told *Printer's Ink,* the advertising magazine, "and I give the credit for our success to the Ohrbach's campaign. We'd get phone calls: 'Are you the agency for Ohrbach's? How about handling our account?'" Clients who came to him because of his Ohrbach's advertising were more easily able to accept his originality when it came to their own advertising. This group includes Levy's, Polaroid, El Al, and Volkswagen. Those clients who

I found out
about
Joan

The way she talks, you'd think she was in Who's Who. Well! I found out what's what with *her*. Her husband own a bank? Sweetie, not even a bank *account*. Why that palace of theirs has wall-to-wall *mortgages!* And that car? Darling, that's horsepower, *not* earning power. They won it in a fifty-cent raffle! Can you imagine? And those clothes! Of course she *does* dress divinely. But really...a mink stole, and Paris suits, and all those dresses...on *his* income? Well darling, I found out about that too. I just happened to be going her way and *I saw Joan come out of Ohrbach's!*

Ohrbach's

© 1958 by Ohrbach's Inc.

34TH ST. OPP. EMPIRE STATE BLDG. · **NEWARK** MARKET & HALSEY · "A BUSINESS IN MILLIONS, A PROFIT IN PENNIES"®

Plate 20

could not accept his work were asked to leave. "We resigned the Necchi Sewing Machine account even though at the time it was seventy-five per cent of our business," says Robert Gage. "They simply would not let us do things our way."

Ohrbach's is by no means a large account at the agency, billing about $1 million in 1969. And, taken as a whole, the advertisements now being done are no longer startling or even particularly original. They rarely stand out even among the ordure that still passes for retail advertising. Nevertheless, they pointed the agency in the right direction during the most crucial years of its life, and they helped insure its growth and influence over the entire advertising business.

El Al Airlines

Some of Doyle Dane Bernbach's best work has been done for its smallest accounts. Perhaps the knowledge that $10,000 for one newspaper ad is one-third of the year's total budget makes the agency concentrate just that much harder. Perhaps it becomes a challenge to make one's only ad into the supreme sales message, the award-winner's award winner, the magic phrase that turns the whole world into a mass of quivering customers.

Of course this attitude is unrealistic; in certain cases the advertising is a triumph if, as with Levy's, it merely keeps the client from bankruptcy. In other cases, for example with most of the foreign-flag airlines serving the United States, profit is secondary to the prestige at home of running one's planes to America. El Al Israel Airlines, one of the smallest of all, flies to only a few cities in Europe, and in this country only to New York, and has no real hope of expanding its operations here. Even the best advertising could not enlarge its service area.

Knowing this, Bernbach still created a campaign so good that its first two ads revolutionized all airline advertising. The first one ran in *The New York Times* on December 11, 1956. Written by Bernbach and designed by William Taubin *(Plate 21)*, it announced that El Al was putting into service the first jet-prop airliners to be used on the North Atlantic run (Bristol Britannias). They would cut flying time to Europe by two and a quarter hours because the new planes didn't have to refuel at Goose Bay, Labrador, or Gander, Newfoundland. Passengers long accustomed to starting and ending their vacations or business trips with twelve hours of propeller drone and vibration now had at least one reason

On
Dec. 23
the
Atlantic
Ocean
became
20%
smaller

The first jet-prop
in transatlantic service,
El Al's new Bristol Britannia,
flies you to
London 2¼ hours faster
than ever before.

See your travel agent or El Al Israel Airlines, 610 5th Ave., N. Y. 20, PL 1-3400. Also Philadelphia, Chicago, Los Angeles, Montreal

EL AL
ISRAEL AIRLINES

Plate 21

© 1958. EL AL ISRAEL AIRLINES LTD.

NO GOOSE

NO GANDER

No refueling stops at Goose Bay, Labrador or Gander, Newfoundland when you fly El Al jet-prop Britannia between New York and London or Paris. It's the only jet-powered airliner that makes it non-stop regularly across the Atlantic. Book El Al Britannia to London, Paris, Rome, Zurich, Athens, Tel Aviv. See your travel agent or **EL AL ISRAEL AIRLINES,** 610 Fifth Ave., New York 20, PLaza 1-7500.

Plate 22

We don't take off until everything is Kosher.

Kosher is sort of slang for "A.O.K."

Literally, it means "fitting and proper" in Hebrew.

And we take it very literally indeed.

Before we let one of our Boeing 707's off the ground, our crews do some fancy footwork to make sure that everything is just so.

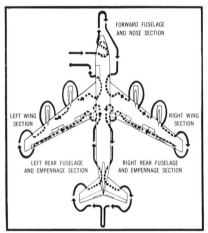

We spend more time walking than flying.

To begin with, the ground crew takes a nice long walk all around the plane. Every inch of the wings, the fuselage and the engines gets scrutinized.

The things that are supposed to be open, are opened.

The things that are supposed to be closed, are closed.

Every item on a very long checklist must be initialed one by one, and the man who checks the checker must sign the completed form.

When the walk is over, the work has only begun.

One member of the ground crew goes into the cockpit to test all the controls. Another man stays outside to see what happens.

They speak to each other in a language all their own. When the man inside turns the control wheel to the right, the man outside says, "Left inboard ailerons up, tabs down, left spoilers up, right spoilers down, right inboard ailerons down, tabs up."

There are even tests to test the tests. Horns blow and lights light to show that things are working properly.

And if something isn't Kosher, everything stops until everything is.

If you took care of your car this carefully once

We check 597 controls...

...one at a time.

a month, it would probably last forever.

Every EL AL jet gets the full treatment twice a day.

Meanwhile, there's the little matter of whipping up 3 square meals for 152 guests of this flying hotel.

What a job that is! Especially when you can't run out to the store if you're missing something at the last minute.

So we make sure that there's a little extra of everything; it hurts us to think of anyone going away hungry or thirsty.

We stock more than a dozen kinds of liquor on board, plus cigars, cigarettes, playing cards, olives, onions and cherries.

There's almost no end to the variety of things: from diapers to 2 sizes of doilies to 3 sizes of paper cups.

We even have 2 kinds of toothpicks: 1 kind for picking hors d'oeuvres and the other kind for picking teeth.

All of which brings us to the basic definition of Kosher that has to do with food.

Since we're the Israeli airline, we cook in the great Jewish tradition.

And the great Jewish tradition includes some tasty morsels like matzo ball soup, kreplach, and gefilte fish that are usually served only on festive occasions.

But we figure that an EL AL trip is a festive occasion all by itself, so we go all out and bend the rule a little by serving them every day.

Actually, the dietary laws can get pretty in-

volved, but what it boils (or broils or roasts) down to is that we don't mix meat and dairy products during the same meal.

So there won't be any butter for your bread with the sumptuous roast beef or leg of lamb, and there won't be cream with your coffee afterward.

On the other hand, when breakfast comes, you'll find gobs of butter to go with your lox, bagels and cream cheese, enough milk to bathe in, and all the cream you want for your coffee.

Hold it! Something isn't Kosher.

Above all, you get to fly with a bunch of enthusiastic people who don't have to work at being hospitable because that's the way they were brought up.

And you can be doubly sure that everything's Kosher. Inside the plane and inside you. EL AL Israel Airlines, 610 Fifth Ave., New York 20, N.Y. PLaza 1-7500.

Plate 23

Plate 24

My son, the pilot.

by Tillie Katz

Believe me.

I'm not saying this just because he's my only son.

But who ever thought a boy from Jacksonville, Florida would grow up to be the Chief Pilot for a whole airline?

It's funny, but Bill wasn't even interested in flying when he was young. Which was all right with me. Frankly, it made me a little nervous even when he played football.

Then something got into him. Just when we all thought he was going into some nice business, he enlisted in the Air Corps.

Pretty soon, he was a group commander with the 8th Air Force in Europe. By the time he came home, it was *Captain* Katz.

With a Distinguished Flying Cross, if you please.

Afterwards, it was flying, flying, flying.

I don't know if you could call him a pioneer or anything, but he was right there when EL AL was only a tiny little airline.

And now? Now you can call him Chief Pilot.

And does he keep an eye on that airline!

Sometimes I think he worries about it too much.

Do you know how many miles he's flown? Over 2 million! Do you know how long he's spent in the air? Over 12 thousand hours!

But if that's what it takes to make the airline so good, that's what he does.

The other pilots even tell a joke on him. They say he only comes down to collect his pay.

But *I* know better. I have two beautiful grandchildren who live in Israel with Bill and my daughter-in-law.

They come to see me now and then, but I wish I could spoil them more often. It's a good thing they have Bill for a father. He spoils everybody. Except himself.

So if you fly on EL AL and see him, tell him I said to dress warm.

to fly El Al, while before, unless they were professional Jews, they had none. The coup was unusually dramatic because it came from such a small airline, one considered most unlikely to make that kind of advance. The second ad was designed by Taubin and written by William Ryder, and it was just as succinct *(Plate 22)*.

These two ads typify the agency's ability to set a tone with a campaign's

WHY IS THIS AIRLINE DIFFERENT FROM ALL OTHER AIRLINES?

1. On all other airlines, you eventually get to Israel, after your plane has stopped in 2 or 3 other places. On this airline, you fly non-stop to Tel Aviv from New York. We're the only airline that flies non-stop to Tel Aviv. (Of course, we fly to 16 cities in Europe, Africa and Asia, too.)

2. On all other airlines, if you hanker for home-made chicken soup, chances are you'll have to settle for bouillon. On this airline we serve only kosher food. Jennie Grossinger herself tells us how to make it delicious. What's so exciting about kosher food? Ever taste a kosher Medaillon de Veau Zingara with truffles?

3. On all other airlines, the stewardesses have painted-on smiles. They grin all the way to Europe. On this airline, our genuine Israeli stewardesses smile when it's meaningful. Like when they're describing the bounty in an antique shop in Jerusalem. Or singing a Hebrew lullaby to a little baby passenger. They're gifted young women. The kind you don't see every day.

4. On all other airlines, the passengers sit like passengers. Moody. Reserved. On this airline, they talk to each other. Loosen up and break matzo, maybe for the first time. They laugh a lot. More like people than passengers. The minute they climb aboard, it's a universal wedding.

ELAL אל על

If this is what Israel's airline is like, imagine what Israel herself is like. Plan to fly there for Passover? Better let your travel agent know right away.

Plate 25

first advertisement that other writers and art directors can expand on almost indefinitely, without resorting to the uneasy imitation that has plagued other imaginative admakers—notably David Ogilvy—when others take over their work.

Before these ads appeared, airlines had wasted millions of dollars over the years reproducing their timetables or their rate schedules in local

51

Take El Al's "passover" flight to Tel Aviv.

Pass over London, Paris, Rome and Athens.
Only El Al flies non-stop from New York to Tel Aviv. (Our Flight 200 leaves every Thursday at 8:00 P.M.)
 Or if it's London, Paris, Rome or Athens you want to go to, don't go away.
 We have stop flights leaving every day but Friday, and those are the stops.
 El Al also flies between more than a dozen other cities all over Europe, Africa and the Near East.
 We wouldn't blame you for being surprised that El Al goes to Nairobi.
 In Nairobi, some people are surprised we go to New York.

For reservations, call your travel agent or PLaza 1-7500.
EL AL Israel Airlines, 610 Fifth Ave., New York 20, N.Y.

Plate 26

We've been in the travel business a long time.

In the beginning, it was sink or swim.
We swam.
Until about 15 years ago when we started to fly.
In 1948, we had one used DC-4, two ex-war aces and plenty of doubts.
Now we have a whole fleet of new Boeing 707 and 720-B jets.
We also have multitudes of pilots (including one named Noah) and no more doubts.

We fly one of the world's longest non-stop flights: New York to Tel Aviv.
The shorter EL AL non-stop flights (New York to London, Paris and Rome) are simply milk-and-honey runs to us.
One thing in particular that tickles us is that nobody notices when an EL AL jet puts down in Athens or Zurich or Istanbul.
It's absolutely routine.
We fly to all the places in the world you'd expect: Brussels, Vienna, Munich,

Amsterdam, Frankfurt.
And we stop at some others that you might not expect: Teheran, Nairobi, Nicosia and Johannesburg.
At close to 600 miles an hour, there are very few places we can't get you to in 6 or 7 hours.
Think where we could get you in 40 days and 40 nights.
Call your travel agent or us at PL 1-7500.

Plate 27

newspapers, sometimes adding sex appeal with a photo of a stewardess pointing to the schedule, even though at that time fewer than one American in ten had ever flown in an airplane. (Only Pan Am, of all the major airlines, had had an advertising program that was at all intriguing or believable.) After these ads, however, the best of the airline agencies were freed from old stereotypes, and were able to use imagination and taste in their work. Eastern Air Lines (Young & Rubicam) and Braniff Airways (Jack Tinker, then Wells, Rich, Greene) began in the 1960s to do intelligent, imaginative, often exquisitely beautiful work. For Bernbach, there was an additional benefit: as a result of the El Al campaign, he acquired in 1961 the American Airlines account, which at a budget of $6 million a year was about fifteen times what he got from El Al.

Although El Al does only a few advertisements each year, and although the vast majority of its customers in the United States are Jewish, it has held its own against the larger carriers, with their greater frequency of service and wider choice of cities served (an important sales point for travelers wishing stopover privileges).

There is some reason for the ethnic slant in El Al ads *(Plates 23–27).* "Flying El Al," says Robert Levenson, copy supervisor on the account (and nephew of Sam Levenson), "is *not* like flying on any other airline. I remember one night flight, sleeping in my seat. As morning came I was awakened by this strange droning sound, and I couldn't place it at first. Then I saw where it came from. It came from a *minyan* of Jews, at the front of the cabin, *davening* against the bulkhead"—something you are not likely to encounter on Pan Am.

Levy's

Once upon a time there was a little Jewish bakery in Brooklyn. For thirty years it quietly sold bagels, onion rolls, and challah to the faithful. Then, trying to expand, it went into packaged ryes, pumpernickel, raisin bread and other goyishe styles. Jews stopped buying and gentiles didn't start. Things went from bad to worse until one day came bankruptcy.

The bank appointed a man named Whitey Rubin as receiver, in hopes of turning the business around. Mr. Rubin, an admirer of Ohrbach's advertising, asked Doyle Dane Bernbach to take on the account, with a budget of $40,000 for 1949, the first year. "We want to get our Jewish customers back," he said.

Bernbach tasted the packaged breads and said, "Mr. Rubin, no Jew would eat your bread. If you want more business, we have to advertise to the goyim."

Plate 28

Are you buying a bread or a bed?

If you're buying white bread strictly by feel, you may be surprised by a few hard facts about "soft" breads. In the first place, it's a fact that the softest bread isn't necessarily the freshest. And it's also a fact that white bread without much body may be white bread without much nourishment. Bread that's a real food ... packed solid with nutrition ... is just bound to be fine, firm, and upstanding, with a texture that won't cave in under the butter knife. So why just feel around for good white bread? Dig deeper. Check the wrapper. Has the baker used unbleached flour? And wheat germ for nature's own goodness? And whole milk (instead of skim milk) for extra richness and nourishment? And pure golden honey (instead of sugar) to lift both the flavor and the energy quotient? If the wrapper says he has, you're getting your family really *good* white bread ... and chances are it's Levy's Oven-Krust!

Levy's Oven-Krust White Bread is oval-shaped, baked slowly on open stone hearths for through-and-through goodness. You'll find it wherever Levy's famous Sour Rye and Pumpernickel are sold. Hear nutritionist Carlton Fredericks recommend it over Station WMGM, 9 to 10 A.M., Monday through Saturday. Henry S. Levy & Sons, Inc., 105 Thames Street, Brooklyn. HYacinth 7-2700.

LEVY'S *oven krust* WHITE BREAD

And so they did. Instead of buying space in the *New York Post* (the *Jewish Daily Forward* of the assimilated), they placed their ads in the *World-Telegram* and the *Journal-American,* two papers whose daily food sections generally featured new recipes for pork roasts. Levy's ads were aimed at that crowd, New York's army of Wonder Bread eaters *(Plates 28, 29).* They are early examples of Phyllis Robinson's ability to express in a phrase the essential qualities of a product. Although visually the ads now

Plate 29

is his bread
a filler-upper

or a builder-upper

Does he fill his empty tummy with bread that's short on nourishment . . . the solid nourishment he needs for a head start on health? It's up to you, mom, to see that every bite your child eats is a builder-upper, not just a filler-upper. So next time you buy a loaf, make sure it contains unbleached flour with wheat germ added . . . the flour formula that actually goes nature one better. Make sure it gives your child, not just skim milk, but whole milk with a 26% butter-fat content . . . as rich in vitamins and minerals as the milk you pour in his glass. Make sure there's honey instead of sugar, so he'll get the energy he needs *plus* a delightful new flavor he'll love. And it's so easy to make sure, mom! Just *check the wrapper.* If it's the red-and-yellow wrapper that says LEVY'S OVEN-KRUST WHITE BREAD, you'll be giving your youngster bread that's packed solid with nutrition . . . and extra flavor too!

Look for Levy's in the oval loaf
wherever Levy's Sour Rye
and Pumpernickel are sold.
Baked by Henry S. Levy & Sons, Inc.,
105 Thames St., Brooklyn.
HYacinth 7-2700

LEVY'S *oven krust* WHITE BREAD

look cheap and dated, the copy remains as interesting to read now as it was then.

Sales improved, but the large grocery chains would not stock Levy's until, a few years later, Mrs. Robinson wrote a radio campaign featuring the voice of a little boy asking for "Wevy's Cimminum Waisin Bwead," while his mother tries to correct his pronunciation. People all over New York walked around saying, "I Wuv Wevy's." It was one of the first radio

You don't have to be Jewish

to love Levy's
real Jewish Rye

Plate 30

You don't have to be Jewish

to love Levy's
real Jewish Rye

Plate 31

You don't have to be Jewish

to love Levy's
real Jewish Rye

Plate 32

campaigns to use the sounds of speech effectively and humorously and, together with a print ad showing a grocer cowering in the corner of his store against a barrage of packages thrown by irate customers, and saying, "All right, already. I'll stock Levy's," finally cracked the big chain-store market for the company.

In 1960 the first of Levy's famous subway posters appeared, with a slogan that came to be one of the most famous in the advertising business: "You don't have to be Jewish to love Levy's" *(Plates 30–32)*. Since Jewish foods are often thought by gentiles to be delicious, and since Jews weren't buying Levy's anyway, the ad had a great effect on sales. It also had an effect on other advertising agencies, some of whom copied the line for their own products, much as they later copied "We're only No. 2" and "We try harder" when they saw the Avis ads. In the great home-decorating-poster boom of the 1960s, Godfrey Cambridge eating a corned beef sandwich stands near the top in sales.

These advertisements obviously create an image of a company named Levy's, and of the bread it makes, but the image is not based on logic, facts, or information. The advertisements ask people who like the ads to buy the bread because they like the ads—not out of gratitude to Levy's for running them (an attitude that has never been successful in American advertising), but because they represent a company that makes eating bread a pleasure.

It is this ability to substitute emotion for logic—or to deal in a logic of pleasure—that distinguishes Doyle Dane Bernbach and its descendants from even the best of the traditional agencies. Jack Tinker's campaign for Alka-Seltzer, for example, beginning in 1965, dealt only with the emotions of upset stomachs and the pleasure of relief from them. There was nothing about formulas, comparatives with other antacids, or method of action. It was *presumed* that the viewer knew the product would work; it was not necessary to convince him. The commercials used humorous abstractions of real-life situations to make their point, and the point was that Alka-Seltzer is associated with emotional relief; the advertising charmingly supplied the image of that relief, and by extrapolation in the viewer's mind the product took on that image.

Wells, Rich, Greene's famous Benson & Hedges campaign began with the fact that there are more puffs in a 100-millimeter cigarette than there are in the more common 85-millimeter length. But instead of trapping itself in hollow claims of more "pleasure," more "coolness," more "taste," and other such vacuous inanities, the agency used the concept of time inherent in greater length, and created a series of vaudeville comedy blackouts that illustrate people losing or gaining time because they are smoking Benson & Hedges.

This is not to say that reason and logic are abandoned in the new advertising. If anything, there is greater honesty, and a greater respect for truth, than was common in the past. There is a refreshing lack of pretense in the advertising of Volkswagen, Volvo (Carl Ally, then Scali, McCabe & Sloves) and Xerox (Papert, Koenig, Lois), because they are based on a recognition that the products are not all that important in the real world, and so honest advertising for them makes their claims even more believable.

The new advertising has been accused of sacrificing salesmanship to humor, of making the television commercial or print advertisement an end in itself; but that attitude underestimates the sophistication of the admakers: they are unwilling to lie about their products. And sales figures show that for the most part these agencies sell their products better than they were being sold before. Sales points are not neglected or omitted in the ads; they are simply being properly used.

What Doyle Dane Bernbach did for Levy's was to recognize that the bread had no discernible characteristics that might set it off from its competitors, no advantages of flavor, nutrition or appearance that might make for good advertising claims. Instead of claiming virtues where there were none, the agency gave Levy's a personality different from that of its competitors—most of which had no personalities at all—and made its name at least recognizable to New Yorkers, if not instantly and universally desirable. This does not automatically ensure that the product will be a success—an agency has little control over that—but without question it can be a great help.

2

Avis vs. Hertz vs. Avis

Avis vs. Hertz

THE BATTLE BEGAN in the Avis camp. An observer tells the story: "Here was Avis, in 1969, *creeping* along, and why they were still in business I couldn't tell you. They had lost money for fifteen consecutive years— fifteen!—and I don't know why they even kept the doors open. If I were the bank, I would have foreclosed, sold off the cars, and taken my loss. But the bank was Lazard Freres, the investment bankers, and they thought they might have a chance to save the company. *I* thought they were nuts."

But that was 1962, and the observer has since changed his mind. Lazard Freres first hired a man named Robert Townsend to run the company, then gave him an absolutely free hand. Townsend, in turn, began a crash program of upgrading Avis from a cheesy, second-rate operation with no reputation at all, and then went after the big money in the rent-a-car business: the corporation executives who rent for business at airports, and who want to be treated like executives instead of potential car thieves.

Townsend went to half a dozen advertising agencies with this request: "I have $1 million to spend, and I need $5 million worth of impact," and was told to get lost. But when he came to Doyle Dane Bernbach, for some quixotic reason Bernbach told him he would do it for him. He asked for ninety days in which to prepare the campaign. "But you must promise to run everything we write without changing a bloody comma. We like to see what we write run, and we don't like to see it get all mucked up in committees. When good advertising goes up there, it gets uncreated." Townsend promised, and then began his waiting period.

Back at the agency, Bernbach, Krone, and copywriter Paula Green took stock of Avis's assets (negligible) and liabilities (enormous). Avis was not the biggest, it was not the best, it was not the most profitable— God knows—nor did it have many of the other attributes common to large corporations. What it did have was Townsend, however, and Krone said later that he felt he could trust Townsend to work like hell at making Avis at least the nicest, friendliest place for a customer to bring his rental business. Given the client, and working from the agency's theory that advertising can act as a tangible attribute of a product, Krone and Miss Green began producing what has been called the most unusual campaign —and the most important—of the 1960s.

Townsend was not quite prepared for it: "They came back ninety days later," he said, "and the campaign looked just awful. I think even *they* were a little dubious. All I had to say was 'Don't run it,' and they wouldn't have [here he may have overestimated himself]. But I must say, the campaign has worked out rather well."

"For Avis," Krone said, "I had to make a new page." The old page, the common print advertisement of the 1950s, was reinvented (in the advertising business, everything turns out to have been done before, generally in the 1920s) by David Ogilvy in 1949. It had a big picture, a large headline underneath, and a good deal of body copy at the bottom. "I compose down at the stat house anyway," says Krone, "playing with type sizes and layouts, and for Avis I had to turn the old thing inside out.

64

Avis is only No.2 in rent a cars. So why go with us?

We try harder.
(When you're not the biggest, you have to.)
We just can't afford dirty ash-trays. Or half-empty gas tanks. Or worn wipers. Or unwashed cars. Or low tires. Or anything less than seat-adjusters that adjust. Heaters that heat. Defrost-ers that defrost.
Obviously, the thing we try hardest for is just to be nice. To start you out right with a new car, like a lively, super-torque Ford, and a pleasant smile. To let you know, say, where you can get a good, hot pastrami sandwich in Duluth.
Why?
Because we can't afford to take you for granted.
Go with us next time.
The line at our counter is shorter.

Plate 33

I made a big headline, big copy, and a small picture" *(Plates 33–39)*.

Of course Krone had done more than turn the page inside out; he and Miss Green had turned the advertising world inside out. There were shocked—even enraged—comments from other agencies and advertisers, to the effect that no one in his right mind could do ads like these, could sell his client short, as they felt these did, could blatantly proclaim that here was a company that was only Number 2 in its field. "It's just free

When you're only No.2, you try harder. Or else.

Avis can't afford to relax.

Little fish have to keep moving all of the time. The big ones never stop picking on them.

Avis knows all about the problems of little fish.

We're only No.2 in rent a cars. We'd be swallowed up if we didn't try harder.

There's no rest for us.

We're always emptying ashtrays. Making sure gas tanks are full before we rent our cars. Seeing that the batteries are full of life. Checking our windshield wipers.

And the cars we rent out can't be anything less than lively new super-torque Fords.

And since we're not the big fish, you won't feel like a sardine when you come to our counter.

We're not jammed with customers.

Plate 34

Plate 35

66

Avis needs you.
You don't need Avis.
Avis never forgets this.

We're still a little hungry.
We're only No.2 in rent a cars.
Customers aren't a dime a dozen
to us.
    Sometimes, when business is too
good, they get the short end and aren't
treated like customers anymore.
Wouldn't you like the novel experience of walking
up to a counter and not feel you're bothering somebody?
Try it.
    Come to the Avis counter and rent a new, lively super-
torque Ford. Avis is only No.2 in rent a cars. So we have
to try harder to make our customers feel like customers.
    Our counters all have two sides.
    And we know which side our bread is buttered on.

advertising for Hertz," was the general reaction among traditionalists.
Of course free advertising for Hertz was the last thing it was. Before this,
you had *always* gone to Hertz; but now, standing in line at the Hertz
counter as you always had before, well, you *had* to check Avis, just to see
if the ads were true. Trying Avis instead of Hertz—just once, for kicks—
became a game, and you talked about it with your friends afterwards.
For many executives, renting from Avis became the "in" thing; it showed

Plate 36

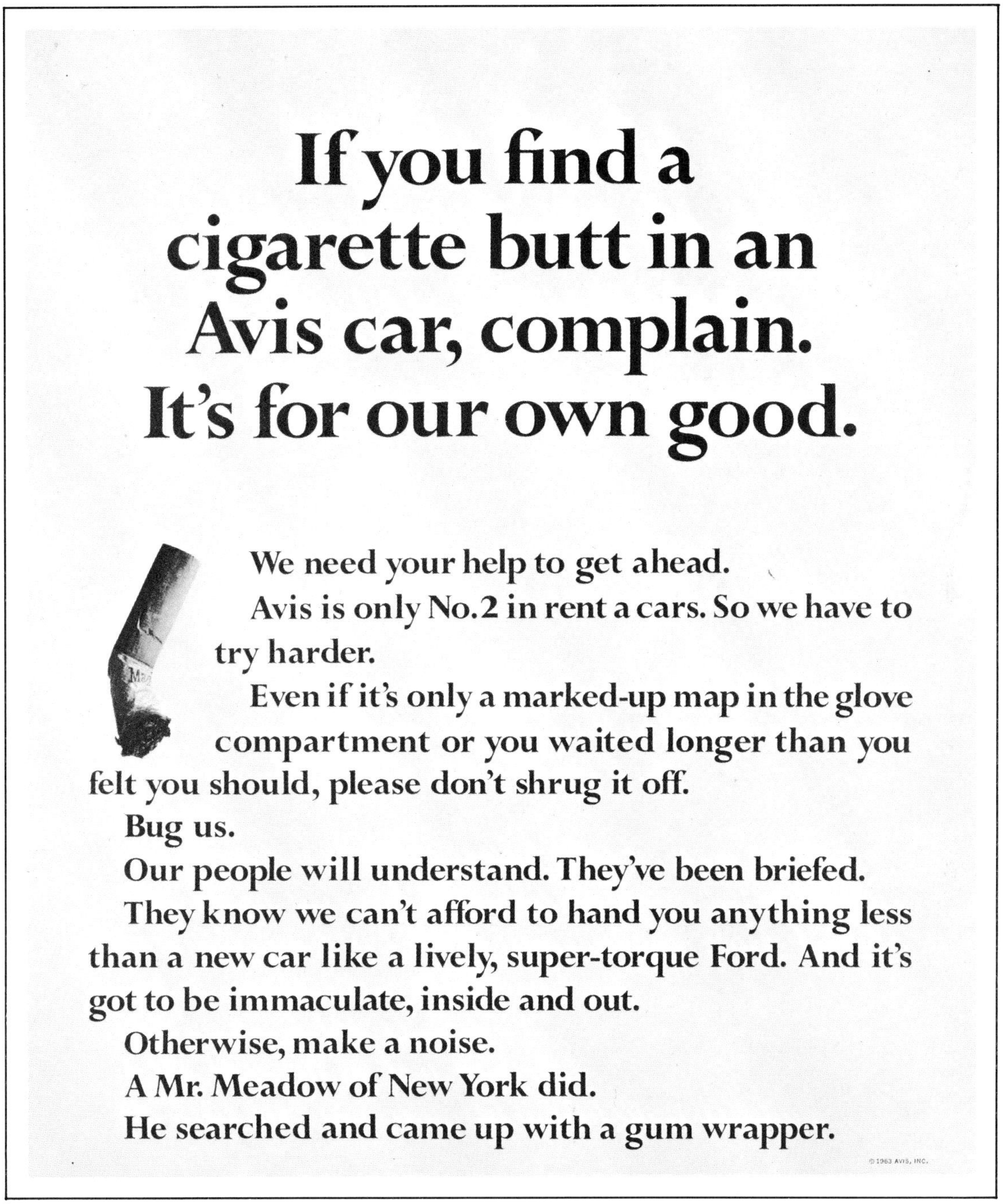

67

If you find a cigarette butt in an Avis car, complain. It's for our own good.

We need your help to get ahead.

Avis is only No. 2 in rent a cars. So we have to try harder.

Even if it's only a marked-up map in the glove compartment or you waited longer than you felt you should, please don't shrug it off.

Bug us.

Our people will understand. They've been briefed.

They know we can't afford to hand you anything less than a new car like a lively, super-torque Ford. And it's got to be immaculate, inside and out.

Otherwise, make a noise.

A Mr. Meadow of New York did.

He searched and came up with a gum wrapper.

© 1963 AVIS, INC.

your identification with the underdog, and perhaps even your appreciation of the ads.

Naturally, if Townsend hadn't made good on his promise to upgrade the company, its personnel, its service, and its fleet of cars, the whole thing would have backfired. But he had a free hand, and he took responsibility for everything the company did. In fact, Krone and Miss Green wrote an ad inviting anyone with a complaint to call Townsend collect, at the

Who do you think of first when you think of rent a cars? Certainly not Avis.

How one of our customers made out his check.

It must be nice to be a household word. Like Jell-O, Coke or Kodak.

But we're not. Avis is only No. 2 in rent a cars, and it's always the big fellow you think of first.

So we have to try harder. Hoping the people who stumble on us will come back for more.

(We probably have the world's most fussed-over Fords. Spick and span and nicely in tune.)

And when someone calls us by the wrong name, we turn the other cheek.

After all, it doesn't matter what you call us.

Just so you call.

© 1964 AVIS, INC.

Plate 37

Avis is only No.2. But we don't want your sympathy.

It hasn't come to this.

Have we been crying too much? Have we overplayed the underdog?

We didn't think so till David Biener, 11 years old, sent us 35¢, saying,"It may help you buy another Plymouth."

That was an eye-opener.

So now we'd like to correct the false impression we've made.

We don't want you to rent Avis cars because you feel sorry for us. All we want is a chance to prove that a No.2 can be just as good as a No.1. Or even better. Because we have to try harder.

Maybe we ought to eliminate the negative and accentuate the positive.

Instead of saying "We're only No.2 in rent a cars," we could say "We're the second largest in the world."

Plate 38

Plate 39

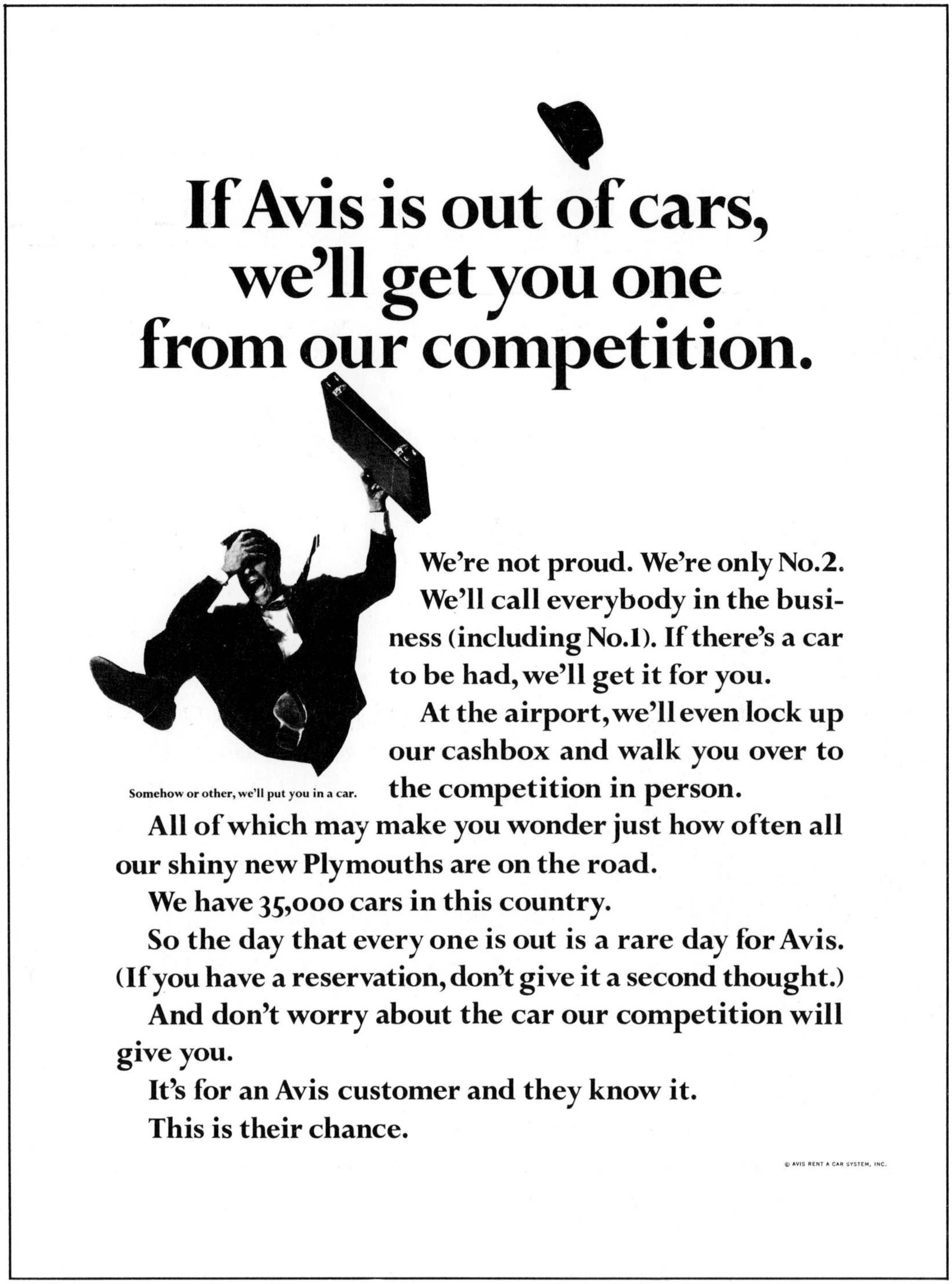

If Avis is out of cars, we'll get you one from our competition.

Somehow or other, we'll put you in a car.

We're not proud. We're only No.2. We'll call everybody in the business (including No.1). If there's a car to be had, we'll get it for you.

At the airport, we'll even lock up our cashbox and walk you over to the competition in person.

All of which may make you wonder just how often all our shiny new Plymouths are on the road.

We have 35,000 cars in this country.

So the day that every one is out is a rare day for Avis. (If you have a reservation, don't give it a second thought.)

And don't worry about the car our competition will give you.

It's for an Avis customer and they know it.

This is their chance.

© AVIS RENT A CAR SYSTEM, INC.

office or at home, and listed his telephone number *(Plate 40).* There were many calls, but all of them were to say how much they liked his company.

For traditionalists, the proof of the campaign's success was of course in the sales figures. In 1962, the year Townsend took over, Avis revenues were $34 million, with a loss of $3,200,000. In 1963, Doyle Dane Bernbach's first year on the account, revenues were $35 million, with a profit—for the first time in fifteen years—of $1,200,000. In 1964, revenues jumped to $44 million and profit to almost $3 million. By 1968 the agency was billing more than $6 million on the account, but in 1969 Avis fired

If you have a complaint, call the president of Avis. His number is CH 8-9150.

If he doesn't answer after 3 rings, try later.

There isn't a single secretary to protect him. He answers the phone himself.

He's a nut about keeping in touch.

He believes it's one of the big advantages of a small company.

You know who is responsible for what. There's nobody to pass the buck to.

One of the frustrations of complaining to a big company is finding someone to blame.

Well, our president feels responsible for the whole kit and caboodle. He has us working like crazy to keep our super-torque Fords super. But he knows there will be an occasional dirty ashtray or temperamental wiper.

If you find one, call our president collect.

He won't be thrilled to hear from you, but he'll get you some action.

© 1964 AVIS, INC.

Plate 40

Bernbach and hired Benton & Bowles instead, probably because of a strikingly inept campaign featuring huge line drawings of bugs attacking Avis's fleet of Plymouths. (It should be pointed out that the campaign was created after Krone was taken off the account; by the summer of 1969 Krone had left Doyle Dane Bernbach to open his own agency.)

An unexpected publicity bonus came when Avis customers, and readers of the ads, began requesting "We try harder" buttons. They sprouted everywhere, the "Kilroy was here" of the 1960s, on football teams, company salesmen, army regiments, college students. It became a catchword —briefly—of believers in the long-gone America of perseverance rewarded. Avis gave away more than $100,000 in pin-on buttons before switching in self-defense to a cheaper, bendable model.

The campaign also had its effect on Hertz, which in 1966 left its old agency and went to Carl Ally Inc. looking for a campaign to stop Avis. It became a battle between the granddaddy of the new advertising (Doyle Dane Bernbach) and its grandson (Carl Ally).

Hertz vs. Avis

The agencies that grew from Doyle Dane Bernbach built their work on Bernbach's premise that advertising is a tangible attribute of a product, as much to be considered in a purchase as price, looks or utility, and not to be thought of simply as a salesman's helper. In this respect they reflect John Kenneth Galbraith's insight that the "new industrial society" has largely eliminated the traditional quality and price differences on which buying decisions formerly were made. Thus, as advertising becomes more important to the purchaser, it then becomes possible to imply that one's product is better than the competition's because one's advertising for it is better. And then, if the advertising really *is* better, sales should improve because the product now has an advantage over the competition: better advertising.

Carrying this another step, one may now *advertise* that his product has better advertising than the competition, with the reasonable expectation that if consumers agree with that, then one's sales will improve. In fact, the Avis–Hertz battle of 1966 turned on precisely that point: whether it was better to advertise that one was the largest company in the field, or that one was *not* the largest company in the field.

Hertz Rent A Car *is* the largest company in the field, and always has been. It has about 50 per cent of a $400 million annual market. The company had been running its "Let Hertz Put You in the Driver's Seat"

For years, Avis has been telling you Hertz is No.1.

Now we're going to tell you why.

We're No. 1 because we're better at helping you get to where you're going.

A car where you need it.

The first step in renting a car is getting to the car. Hertz makes that easier for you to do than anybody else.

We're at every major airport in the United States. And at some airports that are not so major. Ever fly to Whitefish, Montana? Some people do. And have a Hertz car waiting.

No matter how small the airport you fly to, if it's served by a commercial airline, 97 chances out of 100 it's also served by Hertz or by a Hertz office within 20 minutes of it.

We also have locations throughout the downtown and suburban areas of every major city.

And because you don't restrict your travel to city areas, we don't restrict our locations to city areas. We're also out in the country. And out of the country, too. Windy Hill Beach, South Carolina has a population of 100. It has a Hertz office. Chichiri, Malawi in Africa has a population of 2,059. It has a Hertz office.

In all, Hertz has over 2,900 places throughout the world where you can pick up or leave a car. Nearly twice as many as No. 2.

Can't come to us? We'll come to you.

We have a direct-line telephone in most major hotels and motels in the U.S. It's marked HERTZ and it's in the lobby. Pick it up, ask for a car, and we'll deliver one to the door. You often can't get a cab as easily.

What kind of car would you like?

When you rent from Hertz, you're less likely to get stuck with a beige sedan when you want a red convertible. We have over twice as many cars as No. 2.

Not only is our fleet big, it's varied. We do our best to give you what you want. From Fords, to Mustangs, to Thunderbirds, to Lincolns and everything in between.

And because we know that travel can be a bore if you travel a lot, we've even got something to ease your lot. The Shelby GT 350-H. If you know what cars are all about, you'll know what this car is all about.

Who's perfect?

When you rent a new car from us or anybody else, you expect it to be sitting there waiting, ready to go, looking like new.

On that score we claim no superiority over our competition. They goof once in awhile. We goof once in awhile.

Except when we goof it bothers us more because people don't expect the big one to goof. And to make up for it, if our service is not up to Hertz standards we give you $50 in free rentals.* Plus an apology.

No. 2 gives a quarter plus an apology. And advertises that he "can't afford" to do more.

We feel the other way about it. We can't afford to do less.

Besides, the $50 comes out of the station manager's local operating funds. This tends to keep him very alert...and our service very good.

Hot line.

When you're in one city and you're flying to another city and you want to have a car waiting when you arrive and you want it confirmed before you leave, we can do it for you. Instantly. In any one of 1,038 U.S. cities. No other rent a car company can make that statement.

The major reason we can do it is because we recently installed one of the world's largest private electronic reservations systems.

After all, with the supersonic jets in sight and one hour coast to coast flights in prospect, you'll need some quick answers.

We can give them to you today.

About credit.

If you've got a national credit card with most any major company, you've got credit with us.

A businesslike way of doing business.

If you own your own firm or are instrumental in running a firm, you know what a nightmare billing can be.

Have your company rent from us and we'll help ease that nightmare. We can even tailor our billing cycle to fit your paying cycle.

We'll bill by the rental, by the month, by division, by department, by individual, and by blood type if it'll help you.

And now about trying hard.

No. 2 says he tries harder. Than who?

©HERTZ SYSTEM, INC., 1966

Hertz

*There's one thing you have to do for us though: fill out our Certified Service form and mail it to our main office in its self-addressed envelope. Upon verification we'll send you $50 in rental certificates by return mail.

Plate 41

campaign, invented by Norman, Craig & Kummel, since 1958. Although the campaign lent itself to innumerable parodies, it had served a good purpose at the start by making millions of people aware that cars could be rented by the hour, day, or week—anywhere—as well as bought. Avis, a distant second in the business, had nothing to lose and much to gain by persuading Hertz customers that things were faster and friendlier over at the Avis booth. It became fashionable to do business with the company that "tried harder."

When Hertz decided to switch agencies and change its advertising, one of the agencies they considered was Carl Ally. "Hertz called us in November of '65," Ally recalled, "and asked if we would take a small piece of their business. We said no. Then in the spring of '66 they came back again. They saw us and some other agencies, and all the other agencies skirted the issue. We came to the point. We diagnosed the sickness. We told them they're making assholes of you.

"For four and a half years Bernbach had been beating the bejesus out of Hertz. Hertz had been needled, humiliated and beaten by Avis. They see the numbers: Avis is going faster than they are. It's embarrassing them. For four and a half years Avis, through innuendo, implied: Hertz cars are full of cigarette butts, Hertz cars are dirty, Hertz cars are dangerous, Hertz employees are surly. Well, if you run that campaign for four and a half years and get no answer, people believe it's true."

Hertz couldn't have picked a better agency than Ally to cure this kind of sickness. Carl Ally is an articulate, combative man who talks and acts like a cross between a college English teacher (which he was) and a pool hustler (which he also was, though he defers in this area to his partners Jim Durfee and Amil Gargano, who supervise copy and art, respectively and even interchangeably, at the agency). The three of them came out of the Detroit pool halls and into the advertising business by way of Campbell-Ewald, Detroit's largest agency. Ally went to Papert, Koenig, Lois as account supervisor on Xerox, where he was responsible for much of that extraordinary campaign, while Gargano suffered a while at Benton & Bowles before he and Durfee joined Ally in the summer of 1962 to form their own agency. Their first account was Volvo, the Swedish automobile, which they got by presenting to the prospective client a series of advertisements, sketched in rough form by Gargano, in each of which he misspelled the client's name as "Valvo." Although Volvo left in 1967 on bad terms ("I hate to be whipped by ants," said Ally at the time. "It's bad for my people at the agency."), their advertising campaign was in many ways comparable only to Doyle Dane Bernbach's campaign for Volkswagen, and some of it was better.

All of Ally's best advertising has a pungency and personal tang that seems a cross between the best of Bernbach and the best of Howard

If you were in the car rental business and you were No.2 and you had only half as many cars to offer and about half as many locations at which to offer them, and fewer people to handle everything, what would you say in your advertising?

Right.Your ashtrays are cleaner.

Hertz
(Who's perfect?)

Plate 42

Hertz has a competitor who says he's only No. 2.

That's hard to argue with.

Hertz	No. 2
1. A car where you need it.	**1. We try harder.**
We're in big towns like yours. In little towns like Whitefish, Montana. We're at every major airport in the United States and at most of the smaller ones. In fact, if an airport is served by a commercial airline, 97 chances out of 100 it'll also be served by Hertz. Or by a Hertz office within 20 minutes of it. In all, we have over 2,900 places throughout the world where you can pick up or leave a car. Nearly twice as many as No. 2.	
2. What kind of car would you like?	**2. We try harder.**
When you rent from Hertz, you're less likely to get stuck with a beige sedan when you want a red convertible. We have over twice as many cars as No. 2.	

We have Fords, Mustangs, Thunderbirds, Lincolns and everything else in between.

Hertz	No. 2
3. Who's perfect?	**3. We try harder.**
When you rent a car from us and our service is not up to Hertz standards—if we goof—we give you $50 in free rentals.* Plus an apology. No. 2 gives you a quarter. Plus an apology.	
4. Hot line.	**4. We try harder.**
When you're in one city and you're flying to another city and you want to have a car waiting when you arrive and you want it confirmed before you leave, we can do it. Instantly. In 1,038 cities. No other rent-a-car company can do this. The major reason we can do it is because we recently installed one of the world's most advanced reservations systems.	
5. No. 2 says he tries harder. Than who?	**5.**

*THERE'S ONE THING YOU HAVE TO DO FOR US THOUGH: FILL OUT OUR CERTIFIED SERVICE FORM AND MAIL IT TO OUR MAIN OFFICE IN ITS SELF-ADDRESSED ENVELOPE. UPON VERIFICATION WE'LL SEND YOU $50 IN RENTAL CERTIFICATES BY RETURN MAIL. ©HERTZ SYSTEM, INC., 1966

Plate 43

No. 2 says he tries harder.

Than who?

We wouldn't, for a minute, argue with No. 2. If he says he tries harder, we'll take him at his word.

The only thing is, a lot of people assume it's us he's trying harder than.

That's hardly the case. And we're sure that No. 2 would be the first to agree.

Especially in light of the following.

A car where you need it.

The first step in renting a car is getting to the car. Hertz makes that easier for you to do than anybody else.

We're at every major airport in the United States. And at some airports that are not so major. Ever fly to Whitefish, Montana? Some people do. And have a Hertz car waiting.

No matter how small the airport you fly to, if it's served by a commercial airline, 97 chances out of 100 it's also served by Hertz or by a Hertz office within 20 minutes of it.

In all, Hertz has over 2,900 places throughout the world where you can pick up or leave a car. Nearly twice as many as No. 2.

Can't come to us? We'll come to you.

We have a direct-line telephone in most major hotels and motels in the U.S. It's marked HERTZ and it's in the lobby. Pick it up, ask for a car, and we'll deliver one to the door. You often can't get a cab as easily.

What kind of car would you like?

When you rent from Hertz, you're less likely to get stuck with a beige sedan when you want a red convertible. We have over twice as many cars as No. 2.

Not only is our fleet big, it's varied. We do our best to give you what you want. From Fords, to Mustangs, to Thunderbirds, to Lincolns and everything in between. Including the rather fantastic Shelby GT 350-H.

Who's perfect?

When you rent a new car from us or anybody else, you expect it to be sitting there waiting, ready to go, looking like new.

On that score we claim no superiority over our competition. They goof once in awhile. We goof once in awhile.

Except when we goof it bothers us more because people don't expect the big one to goof. And to make up for it, if our service is not up to Hertz standards we give you $50 in free rentals.* Plus an apology.

No. 2 gives a quarter plus an apology. And advertises that he "can't afford" to do more.

We feel the other way about it. We can't afford to do less.

Besides, the $50 comes out of the station manager's local operating funds. This tends to keep him very alert...and our service very good.

Hot line.

When you're in one city and you're flying to another city and you want to have a car waiting when you arrive and you want it confirmed before you leave, we can do it for you. Instantly. In any one of 1,038 U.S. cities. No other rent a car company can make that statement.

The major reason we can do it is because we recently installed one of the world's most advanced reservations systems.

After all, with the supersonic jets in sight and one hour coast to coast flights in prospect, you'll need some quick answers.

We can give them to you today.

About credit.

If you've got a national credit card with most any major company, you've got credit with us.

About rates.

You can rent a car from Hertz by the day and the mile, by the weekend, by the week, by the month, by gift certificate, by revolving credit, by sundry other ways in between.

We offer all these rates for two reasons. To stay ahead of competition. To get more people to rent cars.

When you go to rent a Hertz car just tell the Hertz girl how long you want the car and roughly how much driving you'll be doing. She'll figure out the rate that's cheapest for you.

Speak up No. 3.

Is it you that No. 2 tries harder than?

*There's one thing you have to do for us: fill out our Certified Service form and mail it to our main office in its self-addressed envelope. Upon verification we'll send you $50 in rental certificates by return mail.

©Hertz System, Inc., 1966

Hertz

Plate 44

Aha!
You were expecting another get tough with Avis ad.

After being picked at by No. 2 for four years, we got a little irritated. ·

We felt we had to say something about the things that have been implied about us.

Mostly because these things aren't true. And our people who clean, service, deliver and take reservations wanted the

air cleared.

And now that we've gotten the irritation out of our systems, all future advertising will be devoted solely to acquainting you with how reliable, resourceful, helpful and pleasant we are so you'll come in and rent a car from us instead of our dear friends down the street.

Hertz

No. 1 with pleasant new Fords and other good cars.

Plate 45

Gossage, the San Francisco genius who returned "I" and "we" to the ad man's vocabulary. Some of the agency's television commercials for Volvo are masterpieces of the comic film, and would repay serious study by cineastes. (Ally's great dream is to acquire the Preparation H suppository account, for which he has created the slogan: "Up Yours With Ours . . . And Kiss Your Piles Goodbye." It awaits only client approval.)

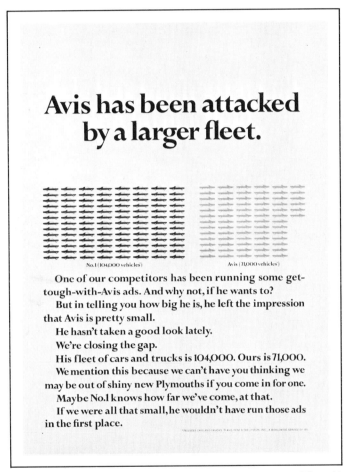

Plate 46

Ally's first ad for Hertz came right to the point: Doyle Dane Bernbach had made a serious contender out of Avis purely through an advertising tour de force, and it was necessary to set the record straight *(Plate 41)*. The first series of ads was designed to restore confidence in Hertz—by its customers, of course, but also by Hertz employees, who had themselves begun to believe the Avis ads *(Plates 42–44)*. Ally ran six advertisements in this vein, all written by Durfee; then, when he felt the point had been made, he capped it with one more *(Plate 45)*.

Plate 47

80

Would you believe Avis is No.1½?

Avis.

Well, in a manner of speaking, we're still No.2.

But technically, we're No.1.5556. After four years of trying harder, we've cut No.1's lead almost in half. (Based on the latest figures from 26 major airports.)

And do you know what happens when you get that close to the top?

Your people try even harder.

Take Ernie Foote, for example.

A customer showed up with an expired out-of-state driver's license. So Ernie took him to the highway patrol for a driver's test. He passed. Got a Mississippi license. And was off in a shiny, new Plymouth.

Obviously, our people are keeping score. And they can smell the pennant.

Why No.1 has to do something about Avis:

No.1   Avis

In 3 years, No.1's share of car rentals dropped from 56% to 50%. Avis' share jumped from 29% to 35%.

You've probably noticed the big change in No.1's advertising lately.

No more jolly man flying into the driver's seat.

Instead, they've come out with a get-tough-with-Avis campaign. Why?

Because No.1's share of the rent a car business is getting smaller.

And Avis' share is getting bigger. (Based on the latest figures from 26 major airports.)

Trying harder is paying off.

Spotless Plymouths, full gas tanks and smiles you can believe have been bringing No.1's customers to Avis.

The trend is clear.

If Avis isn't stopped, we'll be No.1 by 1970.

Plate 48

Plate 49

The harder they try, the better we get.

If you think being number two and fighting to get on top gives you a reason for trying hard, consider being on top and fighting to stay there.

You try harder to hang on to what you've got than you do to get something you never had in the first place.

Which is why Hertz isn't about to be out-tried.

Our soap bill went up $13,000 last year. We've been washing our new Fords a lot.

Our employees have risen to our competitor's challenge. In the last couple of months, we've been swamped with nice letters about Hertz people going to ridiculous extremes to please customers.

A Hertz girl in Oklahoma City sewed a button on a customer's coat.

A Hertz man in Brownsville, Texas took a customer with a toothache to his dentist.

A Hertz man in Greenwood, Mississippi drove five miles to get a quart of milk for a customer with ulcers.

No, Hertz people don't have to do these things.

But when you're number one in rent a cars and have a competitor who's just dying to see you become number two, you do things you don't have to do.

If you have a pleasant experience when you rent from Hertz, don't thank us. Thank our competition.

They're making us so good, they'll never catch us.

Hertz

It's the underdog that's keeping the top dog on top.

This kind of direct attack had been very rare in advertising, one of the unwritten rules of the business being that you never so much as mention your competitor's name in your ads, much less attack him and his advertising, on the premise that this lowers the moral tone of the business. Moreover, no one had ever before attacked Doyle Dane Bernbach, which had come to be regarded as The Father To Us All. But, as Ally said at the time, "You don't get to the top in this business by attacking Kenyon & Eckhardt [an old-line agency]."

Bernbach struck back *(Plates 46–48)*. And Ally counterattacked
(Plate 49).

Advertising commentators began picking at both Avis and Hertz for their campaigns, on the ground that they were talking to each other and not to their customers, but in fact both Ally and Bernbach were quite careful to use the ads to project the companies' images as they wished customers to see them. Hertz was making it clear that no one gets to be Number 1 without deserving to be; and Avis was trading on what it felt to be America's sympathy for the underdog. Both campaigns, however, started from the assumption that the company with better advertising deserved to get more business.

In the spring of 1967 Ally stopped its attack. "Enough was enough," said Durfee. "It was a once-in-a-lifetime situation, and we had made our point."

Was the campaign a success? "Just look at the sales figures," said Ally. "At the end of six months we turned it around." Hertz's share of market, which had dropped from 55 per cent to 45 per cent in the previous four years, rose in six months to 50 per cent. "You might say," he concluded, "that for four and a half years they did the foreplay, and then we came in and rammed it home."

3

David Ogilvy

TWO COPYWRITERS BESTRIDE THE miniworld of advertising like colossi, and have since 1949, when each founded his agency: one is Bernbach, and the other is David Ogilvy of Ogilvy & Mather. Although Bernbach's influence has lately grown stronger than Ogilvy's, with many agencies clinging to his coattails and building on his style and approach to advertising, it was Ogilvy who made the first famous postwar campaigns. Working essentially alone, he created the Hathaway, Schweppes, British Travel Association, Commonwealth of Puerto Rico and Rolls-Royce campaigns. Unlike Bernbach, who always worked with an art director, Ogilvy designed his own page layouts, often chose the photos and type faces, and even picked the media in which to run the ads.

The two men are unalike in other ways. Where Bernbach was a Brooklyn Jew who had made a name for himself as a copywriter long before he formed his own agency, Ogilvy was a Scotsman of titled background, who came to this country in the late 1930s to work as a researcher for George Gallup. When he started his agency, with capital provided by his older brother, a London advertising man, he had never written an advertisement in his life. He intended to be research director of the new agency, but disliked the work of his rather conventional American partner, bought him out, and began writing his own ads.

Ogilvy is probably the best advertising essayist ever to have worked in the United States. He returned literacy, wit, information, and grace of style to advertising (some would say they had never been there before). Clifford Field, an Englishman who for years was Ogilvy's assistant copy chief and writer on the master's pet accounts, says, "David doesn't really have much poetry in his soul. But he's one of the finest austere writers I know."

"When I first began making advertisements," says Ogilvy, "I looked at the so-called mass magazines, and I was impressed by the extraordinary gap between editorial content and advertising content. I saw that the editors were writing with taste to an intelligent audience, and the advertising writers were writing to idiots. I saw no reason why we couldn't treat the consumer as an intelligent person instead of a moron, why we couldn't treat her as the editorial writers did, (though there is a cheat in there, however: most of my early campaigns were written for *The New Yorker.*) But at the time I started, advertising writers had their own lingo, and it was awful. We even invented a slogan in their style, here, as a joke: 'Thrilled with zesty, tangy goodness.' But that was how many of them wrote. And some still do, of course."

In his best years—from 1950 to 1960, after which he withdrew from a good deal of the day-to-day agency work—Ogilvy turned out advertising that was awesomely good, including most of the material reproduced in the next chapters. In those early years, he influenced almost every

CORNELL CAPA

This is a "shock tube" at Shell's Research Laboratories near San Francisco. A high speed camera at the far end allows Shell scientists to study the fundamentals of combustion.

BULLETIN:

Shell discloses the <u>nine</u> ingredients in today's Super Shell—and the remarkable things they do to give your car <u>top performance</u>

Super Shell gasoline, with nine ingredients, is now in St. Louis. Today's formula contains cresyl-diphenyl-phosphate—a new, improved version of TCP. Read how this patented additive increases mileage, releases power, and helps your car give top performance

Today, every Shell dealer in this area has remarkable Super Shell in his pumps.

A notice on each Super Shell pump promises that this gasoline will give your car top performance. Shell's scientists want you to know why they can make this promise.

Ingredient #1 is TCP for power, mileage and longer plug-life

Super Shell now contains an even better version of this famous additive. Its chemical name is cresyl-diphenyl-phosphate.

TCP* additive can give your car up to 15 per cent more power; up to 17 extra miles per tankful; and can make plugs last up to twice as long.

New TCP does this by neutralizing certain harmful effects of combustion deposits. It is scientifically formulated to keep them from glowing when hot—a major cause of power loss. Also to keep them from diverting your spark—a major cause of "missing."

Ingredient #2 is "cat-cracked" gasoline for power with a purr

This is petroleum that has actually *cracked* under 900-degree heat and catalytic action. Its heavier molecules have been shattered into livelier, lighter ones.

The result is a super-octane ingredient that makes your engine purr with power the moment you put your foot down.

NOTE: "Cat-cracking" refers to the use of a catalyst—the mysterious substance that can alter molecules without changing itself.

Ingredient #3 is Alkylate, noted for knock control in hot engines

Jimmy Doolittle helped pioneer this outstanding high-octane ingredient for Shell aviation fuel.

Alkylate—the ingredient that took the dream of 100-octane gasoline out of the lab and put it into the skies—is now in Super Shell. It controls knocking in hot engines at high speeds better than anything else yet available.

NOTE: The engine in your car may frequently turn even faster than the engines of a DC-7 at cruising speed. Think of this next time you are passing on the highway.

Ingredient #4 is anti-knock mix for extra resistance to knocks

You might think that two high-octane ingredients are enough for knock-free performance. But Shell's scientists have ears like musicians.

They insist on adding a special anti-knock mix. A mix, so effective, one teaspoon per gallon can boost anti-knock rating by five points.

This mix has the tricky job of *regulating* combustion so that Super Shell gives each piston a firm, even push—rather than a sharp blow which would cause a knock.

Ingredient #5 is Butane for quick starts on cold mornings

Butane is so eager to get going that Shell keeps it under pressure 400 feet below ground to stop it from vaporizing by itself. Think what this extra volatility means in cold weather. Your engine fires in seconds. There is less strain on your battery. And none on your patience.

NOTE: Super Shell is primed with Butane all year round. In winter, Shell scientists simply increase the quick-start dose.

Ingredient #6 is Pentane mix for fast warm-ups on cold days

Pentanes are made by tearing gasoline apart, much as you split kindling to start a log fire.

In this case, the "logs" are petroleum's heavier hydrocarbons. A special process transforms their molecules from slow-burning "logs" into the quicker-firing "kindling."

NET RESULT: Fast warm-up and top performance in a hurry.

Ingredient #7 is an "anti-icer" to check cold-weather stalling

Super Shell's formula is adjusted as often as eight times a year to beat the weather. For example, whenever the temperature is likely to be less than forty-five degrees, a carburetor anti-icer is added.

Why add anti-icer at forty-five degrees? Because, even then, frost can form in your carburetor just as it does in your refrigerator. It can choke your engine dead.

Ingredient #8 is gum preventive to keep carburetors clean inside

Even the purest gasoline can form gum when stored. This can clog carburetors and foul automatic chokes. But, with Super Shell, you needn't worry. A special gum preventive does the trick.

It acts like a policeman controlling a mob. Regulates unstable elements to help keep them from clotting. Hence no gum problem.

Ingredient #9 is Platformate for extra energy, more mileage

It takes eight million dollars' worth of platinum catalyst for Shell to produce Platformate. But fortunately for you and for us, this precious stuff can be used over and over again.

The platinum re-forming process, which gives Platformate its odd name, converts petroleum into super-energy components—such as benzene, xylene and toluene.

These three alone release 11 per cent more energy per gallon than the finest 100-octane gasoline.

But make no mistake. This is not untamed energy. Far from it. The super-energy of Platformate is harnessed by the eight other ingredients in Super Shell, where it behaves so well you scarcely know it's there. That is until you note your extra mileage. After that, there is no doubt.

Test Super Shell for yourself

Try Super Shell next time you fill up. You'll soon *feel* and *hear* a difference in the way your engine runs.

That difference is *top performance.*

SHELL ®

A BULLETIN FROM SHELL RESEARCH —where 1,997 scientists are working to make your car go better and better.

Shell engineer uses stethoscope to check one of Detroit's latest engines for top performance. Shell scientists, in their continuous study of the proper care and feeding of today's automobiles, use countless other instruments besides. Electron microscopes, X-ray cameras, shock tubes, Geiger counters —and so forth. The knowledge gained leads to constantly improving products. New, improved TCP additive is a result of such research.

*Trademark for Shell's unique gasoline additive. Gasoline containing TCP is covered by U.S. Patent 2889212.

Plate 50

copywriter in America; long-copy advertisements filled magazines and newspapers with page after page of rambling essays couched in an editorial style. Art directors seemed to be left in the lurch as writers forced them into photo-caption-text layouts in the Ogilvy manner. Slowly, though, nature's own remedy began to right the balance. It was discovered that the imitative ads ranged in quality from dull to unreadable, that in fact most American copywriters, like most other Americans, are terrible essayists. "I take great pains with my work," says Ogilvy. "The most effective advertisement I ever wrote was the Beardsley Ruml ad for Puerto Rico [reproduced in that section]. I wrote seventeen drafts. Most writers don't take that trouble."

There is of course much more to Ogilvy than craftsmanship and style. He was able to add an element of fiction to his clients' products, to create fantasies for consumers to associate with them, that seemed to make his clients' products more desirable than their competitors'. And the austerity of his writing made the fantasies more believable. One could identify much more closely with the Man in the Hathaway Shirt than with a man in an Arrow shirt.

In cases where there was no discernible difference between competing products, he would seize on one attribute, fictional or real, and pre-empt it for his client. He never made any bones about this, nor was he disturbed by allegations of immorality for doing so. In 1961 he did it on a monumental scale for Shell Oil Company, using a $15 million advertising budget to list nine ingredients and additives that are put into Super Shell, but neglecting to mention that they are put into every other leaded premium gasoline as well—and further omitting the fact that they are there only because the lead would otherwise foul up the engine *(Plate 50)*.

By 1960 Ogilvy had built his agency into the twelfth largest in the country. But agencies cannot grow for long on the work of one man. Ogilvy demanded imitation, rather than imagination, from his writers, and many of the best ones left for more liberal agencies. Unlike Bernbach, Ogilvy was not a teacher, and had little patience with those who worked in a style different from his own. By the early 1960s the agency seemed to be feeding off its own earlier work, and, in spite of periodic, well-publicized reorganizations of the "creative" departments, much of its advertising had become safe and dreary.

"One of Ogilvy's mistakes," says Field, "was that he threw up his hands about art directors." He did not know how to use them properly in creating advertisements, nor did he trust them to work on their own. When television came, he was unable to make the switch, and for a long time it cost the agency a good deal of business. Ogilvy defined his own problem very well, when he said in 1968: "I am one of the best print writers in Ogilvy & Mather, but one of the worst television writers, so I

[now] keep out of it. Most copywriters are inept in television. They think *words*, when they should be thinking *pictures*. They think *logic*, when they should be thinking *scandal*. They have no sense of theater."

And yet the real beneficiaries of Ogilvy's advertising style have turned out to be not copywriters, and not even his own agency, but art directors, and other agencies. What made Ogilvy's ads work so well, apart from the excellence of their prose, were the layouts he perfected for them, and his ability to choose just the right photo to set off the copy. At a time when painters and illustrators were advertising's kings of the hill, Ogilvy used magazine photographers like Tom Hollyman and Elliot Erwitt, who had gotten their training at *Life;* and he chose dramatic, often moving photos that had an editorial look. Art directors at other agencies, like Gage and Krone at Doyle Dane Bernbach, who were freer than Ogilvy's own people, recognized the power of good photos in a simple, believable layout, and used them for their Polaroid and Volkswagen ads. Because Bernbach and his staff wrote copy in a style that juxtaposed headline and photograph in a kind of visual pun that ran back and forth between the two, the frankness and simplicity of the Ogilvy layout worked well as a framework for their ads. And because this style was essentially visual, Bernbach's writers made the transition to television with little trouble.

Ogilvy is diametrically opposed to Bernbach on the subject of research, and insists that all major advertisements and commercials be tested before they run, recognizing that one value of research lies in using it to defend a proposed campaign before a client. "It is hard for clients to argue with research," he says. "They all use it in their own businesses."

Much of the research is used to test different copy lines. "I wrote 'obsolete' in the headline of our first Dove advertisement," Ogilvy recalls. "Before it ran, I took the precaution of researching it. Three housewives out of four didn't know what it meant, so I changed it to 'old-fashioned.'" But his research is not always the objective test he claims it to be. Ogilvy tested "obsolete" against "old-fashioned," and came out with valid information on the illiteracy of American housewives; but the advertising headline the word was used in—"Now DOVE makes soap old-fashioned"—works with either word. The research was essentially irrelevant to the advertisement. The point was illustrated by his famous line: "People who feel diffident about driving a Rolls-Royce can buy a Bentley for $200 less," a line he never researched, presumably because anyone able to put up $15,000 for a car but unwilling for psychological reasons to buy a Rolls could be expected to know what "diffident" means.

And there are other occasions when he does not use research. He was once asked whether, when he first got the Schweppes account, he thought there might be any American market for a product as peculiar as quinine water. "Of course I did," he said. "There's a market for *any* product.

For beverages, it would range from, say, Coca-Cola at one extreme to, say, potassium cyanide at the other. Now a great many people drink Coca-Cola, and not very many people take potassium cyanide, and they're not likely to take it more than once, but quite obviously it has a certain market. I simply knew that Schweppes would fall somewhere in between."

Schweppes

In 1953 Ogilvy got for his agency the account of Schweppes, Ltd., an English carbonated-drink manufacturer, with the job of introducing it into the American market. The product had four major characteristics: (1) It was almost totally unknown in the United States; (2) Its name was unspellable and almost unpronounceable; (3) It would have to sell at a price 50 per cent higher than any comparable beverage; (4) Its taste was revolting.

Within five years, and without improving its taste at all, Ogilvy had managed to persuade Americans to drink 32 million bottles of his product each year, had changed the national summer drink from the Tom Collins to the gin and tonic, and had made his client (Commander Edward Whitehead, President of Schweppes, USA, Ltd.) one of the most famous men in America. Moreover, when a customer walked into a store or bar to ask for tonic, he automatically got Schweppes, even though Canada Dry had been on the market with its own brand since 1936.

It was probably the best single advertising campaign of Ogilvy's career, and one of the half-dozen most successful in American advertising history. What is more, Ogilvy did it on a budget that was tiny for the beverage field. The budget for 1953, the first year, was $250,000, and it did not exceed $500,000 per year until 1960, by which time sales were running more than 40 million bottles a year.

Tonic, or carbonated quinine water, is a product only the English could love. It was invented 150 years ago by an anonymous Victorian, in some fetid Outpost of Empire, by one of Her Majesty's better Empire Builders, who probably loathed the bitter taste of quinine extract even more than he feared the malaria fever it suppressed. With Victorian genius he dissolved his daily dosage in carbonated water, then masked it with a good shot of gin—on the theory, apparently, that gin was the one liquor that couldn't be ruined no matter what you added to it—thus inventing the gin and tonic. In greatly diluted form (one case supplies the minimum daily quinine dosage), that tonic is just what Schweppes is.

Before Ogilvy got the account, Schweppes had been sold in this country in bottles imported from England, at up to 60 cents for a ten-ounce bottle. By 1952, sales reached sixty thousand cases a year through fancy groceries and quality restaurants, and Schweppes's management decided to try for the mass market. They made a deal with Pepsi-Cola whereby each company would bottle the other's products in its own country, which meant for Schweppes that it could sell here at a price much more competitive with other mixers, particularly Canada Dry's Quinac (then selling at 15 cents for twelve ounces). Schweppes would ship the tonic essence, or syrup, from England to the Pepsi bottlers, who would then add carbonated water and sugar and distribute it along with the rest of their line.

Schweppes insisted on maintaining a price higher than Quinac, partly because of freight charges from England, but primarily in order to maintain a quality image with its old customers. The price was 19 cents for a ten-ounce bottle, with some regional variations.

At first only two Pepsi-Cola bottlers would take on Schweppes: New York and Los Angeles. Advertising was to be placed by the Biow Company, Pepsi's agency at the time and one of the largest in the United States. But by a stroke of good fortune, as S. J. Perelman used to say, the Biow Company had a death convulsion just before the first ads were to break, and it became necessary to find another agency.

The chairman of Schweppes in England, Sir Frederic Hooper, a man who detested Americans, knew Ogilvy through his brother and gave him the account, probably as much for his nationality as for his talent. Ogilvy had then been in business four years, and had already made his reputation with the Hathaway Shirt campaign and the first British Travel Association ads. Both these campaigns showed his ability to invest products with qualities not visible in the competition, and to do it without resorting to the empty slogans and hyperbole so common in advertising of the time.

Hooper was sending Commander Whitehead over to run the American operation, and Ogilvy saw in him the perfect symbol for Schweppes. Handsome, very British, fully bearded in an era when most Americans would not tolerate five o'clock shadow, he could ensure the authenticity of the product and even justify its high price. Ogilvy proposed to Hooper that Whitehead himself should appear in the American advertising; then he had to persuade Whitehead to agree. Whitehead, though a showman and performer himself, refused at first, out of fear, as he said, "of becoming a Mr. Rheingold."

Ogilvy, however, has a fantastic ability to insist on the merit of his own ideas, and then to insist on carrying them through no matter how ludicrous they may appear to others. These were faculties that in later years came to do his agency as much harm as good, since they tended to prevent it from exploring television advertising as freely as it might have.

The man from Schweppes is here

Meet Commander Edward Whitehead, Schweppesman Extraordinary from London, England, where the house of Schweppes has been a great institution since 1794.

Commander Whitehead has come to these United States to make sure that every drop of Schweppes Quinine Water bottled here has the original flavor which has long made Schweppes the *only* mixer for an *authentic* Gin-and-Tonic.

He imports the original Schweppes elixir, and the secret of Schweppes unique carbonation is locked in his brief case. "Schweppervescence," says the Commander, *"lasts the whole drink through."*

It took Schweppes almost a hundred years to bring the flavor of their Quinine Water to its present bittersweet perfection. But it will take you only thirty seconds to mix it with ice and gin in a highball glass. *Then*, gentle reader, you will bless the day you read these words.

P.S. If your favorite store or bar doesn't yet have Schweppes, drop a card to us and we'll make the proper arrangements. Address Schweppes, 30 East 60th Street, New York City.

Plate 51

Will you love Schweppes in December as you did in May?

ABOVE you see, not Nanook of the North and not the Abominable Snowman—but Commander Edward Whitehead, Ambassador from the House of Schweppes in London.

The Commander will tell you that this winter's most fashionable drink is Vodka-and-Tonic. (*All* the rage from coast to coast.) And that no capable barman would try to mix an authentic Vodka-and-Tonic without *Schweppes*.

In one hundred years, nobody has found a substitute for Schweppes bittersweet flavor. A flavor that makes every Tonic drink (Vodka-and-Tonic, Gin-and-Tonic, Rum-and-Tonic) taste so *curiously refreshing*.

And nobody has been able to copy Schweppervescence — those patrician little bubbles that last your whole drink through.

Make sure you get the *original* Schweppes when you ask for it. Tastes as good in December as it did in May!

Plate 52

But at the time Ogilvy knew, probably instinctively, that Whitehead had to do it himself, that it could not be a model, even a perfect double, because people would *know*, somehow, that a fake was being perpetrated. And he knew that Whitehead would be what Ogilvy later came to call "a burr, which a good advertisement leaves stuck onto the mind of the consumer." Whitehead agreed to do it.

The first advertisement showed Whitehead, impeccably dressed and fully bearded, stepping off a BOAC plane with a briefcase in his hand *(Plate 51)*. It was striking to look at and fascinating to read, the hallmark of Ogilvy's best work. It had Whitehead, it had news about an unknown product, it had "Schweppervescence" (another burr to be stuck onto the consumer's mind), and it had a line that said, "Schweppes is the only authentic tonic mixer." The line is another example of Ogilvy's penchant for "pre-empting the truth" for his clients. In England, the product had always been called Schweppes Tonic. In the United States, because of the health associations of the word "tonic," the Food and Drug Administration required that it be called simply quinine water. Ogilvy's line neatly implied the old trade name, and at the same time inferred Schweppes's claim to gin and tonic. Pre-empting the word "tonic" on behalf of Schweppes forced people who wanted Canada Dry instead to ask for it specifically. If you asked for tonic, you got Schweppes. Canada Dry ultimately went to court and compelled Schweppes to stop using the line in its advertisements.

Because of the small budget, and the upper-income market they were aiming for, Schweppes's total media list consisted of *The New Yorker* and *Sports Illustrated*, plus large announcement ads in local newspapers when they went into a new market. Very few agencies at that time had the imagination to concentrate their budgets in so small an area. But Ogilvy and Whitehead are soulmates. They both believe, as Whitehead says, that "What the discriminating do today, the undiscriminating will do tomorrow." They had an expensive product to sell, and they sold it by making people believe it was worth more money than its competitors. As the lady said, it was very well spoken of in the advertisements *(Plates 52, 53)*.

Everyone has been extremely fortunate that the commander, who was forty-five years old when he arrived here in 1953, has aged so gracefully. The beard is grayer, the hair thinner, the skin a bit ruddier, but the man still conveys the same charm, breeding and virility. Whitehead has tried for years to remove himself from the advertising in order to devote his full time to his job, which is running the company in the United States; but the agency has not been able to come up with a good enough replacement, physically or metaphorically, and, although everyone denies it, sales have dropped whenever they try.

Great new fashion: <u>Vodka</u> and Tonic!

TWO YEARS and three brief months ago, Schweppes roving emissary, Commander Whitehead, brought Schweppes Quinine Water to these thirsty shores.

Americans tasted. And discovered *Schweppervescence* — those exuberant little bubbles that tickle the palate and delight the soul. Soon, it became practically *unconstitutional* over here to mix a Gin-and-Tonic *without* Schweppes.

"Now, not content with coining a lively new language," says Commander Whitehead, "I find you Americans are coining new *drinks*. Well, bully for you—I've just tasted my first *Vodka*-and-Schweppes, and I must say it was smashing."

The Commander doesn't know the half of it. Many cities are now reporting a distinct groundswell for *Rum* mixed with Schweppes.

Friend reader, however you take your Schweppes, you can be certain of two things.

One—that the Schweppervescence will last your whole drink through. And two—that you are drinking the original and the authentic Quinine Water. Completely different from the crowd of johnny-come-lately imitations. Yet Schweppes costs only a few pennies more!

Plate 53

Hathaway

If Commander Edward Whitehead was the most famous client in America, probably the most famous model was a dispossessed White Russian baron named George Wrangell. A part-time public relations man, of chronically frail health, he made an occasional living by appearing in advertisements. In 1951 a kind fate brought him to the Ogilvy agency, to be considered as a model for the first Hathaway Shirt advertisement, and for the next ten years he made a wonderful living as the Man in the Hathaway Shirt. ("He was a difficult man to photograph," says Clifford Field, who wrote many of the ads. "He had a tendency to turn blue outdoors.")

It would be hard to overestimate the success of this campaign. Agencies often point to sales figures as a measure of their work: in 1950 Hathaway's sales were under $2 million; by 1969 they were close to $30 million. Or they point to name-recognition: in 1950, it can safely be assumed, less than one per cent of the population had ever heard of the C. F. Hathaway Company of Waterville, Maine. By 1960, according to a survey, more than 40 per cent were acquainted with it. In the clothing business, the number of outlets carrying one's line is important: in 1950 Hathaway had 450 outlets in the United States; by 1962 it was selling its line in more than 2,500. It then sold out to Warner Brothers (foundation garments) for $17 million.

Almost all of this was accomplished by an advertising campaign that ran only in *The New Yorker, Sports Illustrated* and *The New York Times Magazine,* with a budget that never exceeded $600,000 annually during its first ten years. It was Ogilvy's first famous campaign, and it made the agency.

Hathaway hired Ogilvy in 1951, when everybody in the men's clothing business knew that ads are taken only to impress the salesmen and the buyers: every month you ran a page in *Undershirt Wholesaler,* every other month in *Cloak and Suit,* and twice a year in *Esquire.* If you had pretensions, you told the salesmen about the big ad going in *The New Yorker* just before Christmas, and, if you were *really* sincere, you actually ran it.

It was the age of the illustrator: shirts, suits, or underpants were drawn in such painstaking detail that the reader could, if he felt like it, count the stitches per inch in the fabric. The ads often served double duty as catalogue pages, and store buyers made sure they got every stitch they were entitled to. The copy was a fitting match for the artwork: "Spring into Summer in Your Manleigh Tailored Shorts" is a fair example of the genre.

Hathaway had been making men's shirts in Waterville since 1837, and selling them at a few of the highest-priced men's stores. Why, in 1951, they decided to advertise for the first time remains one of the business's minor mysteries. Why they chose the new Ogilvy agency is a greater one; and how they chose it the most mysterious of all. Ogilvy and Ellerton Jetté, who was then president of Hathaway, had a mutual friend through whom Jetté contacted Ogilvy. "You don't know me," he said, "but I would like you to handle our advertising. We cannot spend much money [$30,000 was the first year's budget], but I will promise you one thing: so long as you handle the account, I will not change one word of your advertisements."

"I blanched at the amount," says Ogilvy, "but how can you say no to an offer like that? You can bloody well believe I worked hard on that account."

In describing how the first, famous ad came to be written, Ogilvy recalls: "I had taken from J. Sterling Getchell [a famous advertising man of the 1920s] the idea that every picture in an advertisement should have story appeal. I worked at home, at night, and made a list of eighteen things that might contribute story appeal to the Hathaway ad. The nineteenth was an eyepatch for the model.

"The art director had selected Baron Wrangell to pose for the ad and I approved him. The photography session was to be at a men's store on Madison Avenue. On my way over to the session I stopped in at the drug store and bought a few eyepatches. I walked into the session a little late— they were all waiting for me—and said, 'Here, take a few pictures with this on, and then I'll leave.' When we got the photos back, we knew that they were right." *(Plate 54).*

The advertisement became a conversation piece all over the country, even though it had appeared only in *The New Yorker*. It was parodied in cartoons, joked about at cocktail parties, and posted in men's shops at the shirt counter. Fairfax Cone of Foote, Cone & Belding, in a selection of his ten favorite ads of 1951, said: "This is the first advertisement for Hathaway shirts that I have ever seen. And if there is never another, I shall always remember the name. . . . The copy puts a thin coating of snobbery on a base of dedication—with proof [of the product's qualities]."

Through the years, Jetté kept his promise and never touched a word of the ads. From time to time, he would drop in to chat with Ogilvy.

"Jetté was here one day," recalls Ogilvy, "and in the middle of our conversation he suddenly said, 'Why are you wearing a white shirt? You should never wear a white shirt before sundown.' We went on talking for a few minutes without my realizing what he had said, and then I asked him, 'Why did you say that?' 'Frankly,' he said, 'we can't make a penny on white shirts. We have to move people over to colored shirts.'"

The result was an ad *(Plate 55)* that stated: "Wearing a white shirt is like wearing a uniform . . . a pitiful abdication of individuality." This

The man in the Hathaway shirt

AMERICAN MEN are beginning to realize that it is ridiculous to buy good suits and then spoil the effect by wearing an ordinary, mass-produced shirt. Hence the growing popularity of HATHAWAY shirts, which are in a class by themselves.

HATHAWAY shirts *wear* infinitely longer—a matter of years. They make you look younger and more distinguished, because of the subtle way HATHAWAY cut collars. The whole shirt is tailored more *generously*, and is therefore more *comfortable*. The tails are longer, and stay in your

trousers. The buttons are mother-of-pearl. Even the stitching has an ante-bellum elegance about it.

Above all, HATHAWAY make their shirts of remarkable *fabrics*, collected from the four corners of the earth—Viyella® and Aertex® from England, woolen taffeta from Scotland, Sea Island cotton from the West Indies, hand-woven madras from India, broadcloth from Manchester, linen batiste from Paris, hand-blocked silks from England, exclusive cottons from the best weavers in America. You will get a

great deal of quiet satisfaction out of wearing shirts which are in such impeccable taste.

HATHAWAY shirts are made by a small company of dedicated craftsmen in the little town of Waterville, Maine. They have been at it, man and boy, for one hundred and twenty years.

At better stores everywhere, or write C. F. HATHAWAY, Waterville, Maine, for the name of your nearest store. In New York, telephone OX 7-5566. Prices from $5.95 to $20.00.

Plate 54

"Never wear a white shirt before sundown"

—says Hathaway

HATHAWAY takes the view that no well-dressed man should wear a white shirt before sundown. A white shirt with a business suit is really the loudest thing you can wear. It looks clean in the morning, but by afternoon it gets soiled at the collar and cuffs. This looks awful. Wearing a white shirt at the office is like wearing a uniform—a pitiful abdication of individuality. Gentle reader, you may be wearing a white shirt at this very moment. HATHAWAY has no desire to insult you— heaven knows, we have been making white shirts for 120 years, and expect to go on making them. But we also make patterned shirts, and we would never dream of wearing anything else—before sundown.

Classic stripes, checks, plain colors are so much more interesting. So much more practical. So much better looking. Next time you are in the market for shirts, ask the store to show you some of HATHAWAY's patterned shirts. They are in superb taste, and they are a whole lot better made than ordinary mass-produced shirts. The prices start at $6.95. It isn't every store that stocks HATHAWAY shirts—only the most distinguished in each city.

Write C. F. Hathaway, Waterville, Maine, for the name of your nearest store.

Plate 55

"Men who die intestate are nincompoops," says Baron Wrangell, the Man in the Hathaway shirt. Here he writes a codicil to his will.

"To my son Benjamin–one million dollars and all my Hathaway shirts"

What makes a Hathaway shirt unmistakable–and superior to any ordinary, mass-produced shirt? Hathaway selects the finest fabrics from the four corners of the earth–and takes 77 separate operations to tailor a single shirt.

MORE AND MORE MEN are realizing that it is silly to buy good suits, and then spoil the whole effect by wearing a cheap, mass-produced shirt. Hence the growing popularity of Hathaway shirts, which are in a class by themselves.

The first thing that you will notice about Hathaway shirts is the quality of the fabrics. They feel smoother than run-of-the-mill shirtings. They look more lustrous. They also wear longer – usually a matter of years. Laundering actually improves their appearance and feel.

"There is nothing so luxurious and comfortable to wear," says Ellerton Jetté, Hathaway's chairman, "as a fine cotton shirt that has been laundered from ten to fifty times."

$6.50 to $30

Many of Hathaway's fabrics are imported. Sea Island Cotton from the West Indies. Scotch Broadcloth from David & John Anderson, Ltd. of Glasgow. Viyella from William Hollins Ltd. of Nottingham, near Sherwood Forest. Shantung cotton from Switzerland.

You can spend $30.00 for Hathaway's finest shirt, made of silk hand-woven in India. A good New England broadcloth will cost you about $6.50.

Whatever you pay, you get the same Hathaway workmanship in every Hathaway shirt.

Every collar turned by hand

If you were to go to the charming old town of Waterville, Maine, and visit the Hathaway workrooms, you could talk to cutters and stitchers whose fathers and grandfathers worked all their lives for Hathaway, fussing over every detail.

Like father, like son. Hathaway still turns every collar *by hand*. It is the only way to give a collar a soft, comfortable, natural-looking contour – instead of the stamped-out look that machine-made collars have.

Hathaway cuts every cuff with square corners. This takes extra time. The stitcher has to stop at the corner, give the fabric a right-angle turn, and then resume sewing. Hathaway takes the trouble simply because they think that a square cuff looks better than a curved one. For one thing, it is more masculine.

Hathaway never skimps on fabric. There are about 3,300 square inches of fabric in every Hathaway shirt – enough to give you plenty of room through the shoulders, under your arms, and across your chest.

And Hathaway's shirt tails are cut extra-long, so that they stay tucked in and never bunch up around your waist.

When you look at an ordinary shirt, you can spot the seams. They are usually sewn with a double row of conspicuous stitches. Hathaway sews every seam with *single-needle* stitching. The effect is much tidier. The seams are flatter and stronger.

The stitches are so small that you can scarcely see them. There are twenty-two to the inch – about 30,000 in every Hathaway shirt.

The buttons are big. Says Hathaway's chairman: *"Whether he admits it or not, the average man is somewhat clumsy with his fingers. Big buttons are easy to handle. You don't have to waste time fumbling with them every time you put on a shirt."*

Why the buttons stay sewn on

Hathaway's buttons don't break. They don't get yellow in the laundry. They stay anchored to your shirt because they have three holes, which actually make a more secure "catch" than you ever get from the four holes of the

ordinary button. A paradox – but a fact.

In the illustration below, you see a close-up view of the pocket of a Hathaway striped shirt. Notice how the

pattern matches up perfectly with the pattern on the shirt front – north, south, east, and west.

You will find the same perfect matching of the pattern on every Hathaway stripe and check, because Hathaway's cutters *hand-match* every pocket. It takes extra time, and uses extra material. But anyone with an eye for perfection can see that it's worth it.

Is your collar right for you?

Men who have their shirts custom-made invariably pay particular attention to the cut of the collar. Rightly so. Your collar is always front and center. It either helps your appearance or it doesn't.

That is why Hathaway makes shirts in an unusually large range of collar styles. If your neck is on the short side, you should wear one of Hathaway's *Low-Slope* collars – the London regular or the button-down, for example. These collars sit rather low in front, which has the effect of lengthening your neck and making you look taller.

If you think that your neck looks long enough as it is, wear one of Hathaway's round collars, pin collars, or tabs. These sit a bit higher – but still leave your Adam's apple unpinched. A mercy.

Hathaway pays frequent calls on the world's finest custom shirtmakers to find out what's new among the boulevardiers. Right now, the trend on the Continent is toward collars with somewhat *shorter points*.

It's a simple matter of aesthetics. Those narrow lapels that you see on most of the new suits *demand* proportionately shorter collar points.

Accordingly, Hathaway is now making up shirts with shorter-point versions of several classic collar styles. If

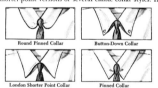

Round Pinned Collar	Button-Down Collar
London Shorter Point Collar	Pinned Collar

you have bought any suits lately, you should look at these new Hathaway shirts. You owe it to your tailor.

Where to buy Hathaway shirts

You will find Hathaway shirts from coast to coast, at stores that keep up the great tradition.

If you don't know of a store near you that carries Hathaway shirts, fill out the coupon below and mail it to Hathaway. No salesman will call.

Plate 56

line drew an irate letter from an army general, furious at the slur on his patriotism.

In 1953 Ogilvy wrote one ad which used the phrase "ineffably male." *Advertising Age,* the weekly newspaper of the business, had a reporter phone a number of advertising people, including Ogilvy, to ask if they knew what "ineffable" meant. Only two were able to define it. One was the advertising manager of *The New Yorker,* which had run the ad; the other was a writer for *Advertising Age.* Ogilvy did not know. "They caught me with my pants down," he commented later. Undaunted, he tried again later that year with the phrase "doyen of New England shirt makers," but missed once more, and from then on the ads used a smaller vocabulary *(Plate 56).*

Surprisingly enough, the success of the Hathaway campaign had little effect on men's-wear advertising in general. In the late 1950s Howard Gossage wrote a famous series of ads in *The New Yorker* for Eagle Shirts —a contest to name shirt colors—which made his reputation if not that of his client; but otherwise the field has remained a haven for hacks.

The reason, certainly, is that a client must want good advertising before he can get it, and he must be able to recognize good advertising before he can want it. Men's-wear manufacturers are notoriously slow learners.

British Travel Association

It has been wisely said that good travel advertising is like good pornography: it gives the reader something worthwhile to think about when he might otherwise be wasting his time in grubbier occupations. So far as is known, David Ogilvy has never written a line of pornography in his life, but he is a master of the escapist fantasy, skillfully masked by stately phrasing.

Ogilvy began writing British Travel Association ads in 1951, then in 1955 turned the campaign over to Clifford Field, who wrote most of the subsequent ads in Ogilvy's style, until he left the agency in 1965.

"When you're writing travel advertising," says Field, "you have an embarrassment of riches in what you can say. A country is a country, after all. You can either pull out all the stops emotionally and write a paean to the country [*Plate 57*], or else you can just give them a hell of a lot of information about the place" *(Plate 58).* It is sometimes possible, however, to combine both *(Plates 59, 60).*

Plate 57

Embark in the shadow of Big Ben, London's favorite clock.

Strand-On-The-Green, one of London's riverside villages.

Hampton Court Palace, showing the Queen's heraldic "beasts."

How to cruise up the Thames from

Once upon a time, the Thames was England's main highway. Kings, nobles, adventurers traveled on it. Where they went, they left *history* behind them.

Take a leisurely trip down nine centuries, and up ninety miles of river, by motor launch from London to Oxford. It will cost you only $55, including all your food and three nights' stay at riverside inns.

You embark in the shadow of Big Ben, and cruise past the Palace of Westminster, home of both Houses of Parliament. Your boat takes you past three other palaces and lands you at a fourth—Hampton Court.

Cardinal Wolsey built it, Henry VIII lived in it, Queen Catherine Howard haunts it.

On through the meadows of Runnymeade, where King John signed the Magna Carta, to Windsor Castle, a

Plate 58

Windsor Castle—the largest inhabited castle in the world.

The "Swan" at Streatley—a friendly riverside inn.

Magdalen Bridge at Oxford. Pronounce it "Maudlen."

London to Oxford—4 days for only $55.

royal fortress-palace for 900 years. (If history makes you *thirsty*, take heart. There's a bar on board your boat.)

At last you come to Oxford, the city of dreaming spires and wide-awake intellects. You *can* get back to London in just an hour by train. But will you, with Oxford spread before you?

Send this coupon for your *free* copy of our helpful new guide, "Vacations in Britain." Fifty-six fact-filled pages, 60 color pictures; just what you need to launch your vacation. Then see your travel agent.

The British Travel Association campaign was the first great travel advertising ever done in the United States. It influenced—for years it overwhelmed—all other tourist campaigns with its evocative prose and its stately, eloquent style. (It was not until 1961, when Doyle Dane Bernbach began its dazzling, totally visual television commercials and print ads for the island of Jamaica, that anyone even tried another approach.)

Young innocence and wicked history at the Bloody Tower

THESE choirboys singing in front of the Bloody Tower are from St. Peter ad Vincula—a Royal Chapel within the Tower of London.

The Bloody Tower is one of *twenty* towers in the Tower of London. Here, in 1483, two little princes are said to have been smothered on the orders of Richard III.

You will be shown around by the Honorary Members of the Queen's Bodyguard of the Yeomen of the Guard (Beefeaters).

You can see two in the picture.

They'll show you the Crown Jewels; the Traitor's Gate; and the block on which two of Henry VIII's wives were beheaded. The surroundings are bloodcurdling, but the Beefeater guides are the friendliest in Europe.

Mail coupon for *another* friendly guide—free 56-page

color booklet "Vacations in Britain." And see your travel agent.

This is a mailing label. Please *type* or use *block letters.*

British Travel, Box 923, New York, N. Y. 10019

TO:

NAME

ADDRESS

CITY ___ STATE ___ ZIP
755

British Travel: New York—680 Fifth Avenue; Chicago—39 So. La Salle St.; Los Angeles—612 So. Flower St.; Toronto—151 Bloor St. West.

Plate 59

Plate 60

RISING SUN INN (14th cent.) You'll find the Rising Sun in Lynmouth, a fishing village in Devon. While in Devon, try the *cider* – but sip it slowly. It's heady stuff. And it costs only 15 cents a pint.

Britain invites you to eight friendly inns —all 400 years old

You can stay in any of them for about $5 a night—including hearty breakfast of country sausages, bacon or kippers.

LORD CREWE ARMS (15th cent.) This Northumberland bar was once the cellar of Blanchland Abbey. Test your skill in one of the pub games: darts (above), shove ha' penny and skittles.

NEW INN (1311 A.D.) Our picture was taken at lunchtime in Pembridge, Hereford. You can lunch off crusty bread, country cheese and ale for about 75 cents. Dinner is seldom more than $3.50.

FALSTAFF INN (1403 A.D.) This inn is just outside the city wall of Canterbury. Chaucer and his fellow pilgrims passed through that gate in 1387, on their way to the Cathedral and Becket's shrine.

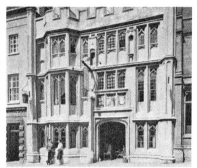

GEORGE AND PILGRIMS INN (1493 A.D.) The local abbot built this inn for pilgrims who came to Glastonbury, "the holyeste earthe in England." The abbot's room has a huge four-poster bed.

BULL INN (c. 1450 A.D.) The Bull in Long Melford was the home of a mediaeval wool merchant. Friendliest way to learn the histories of old inns is to chat with the hosts. No language problem.

FALCON INN (15th cent.) Shakespeare used to live opposite this Stratford inn. *Tip:* Visit Britain's inns in Spring or Fall. Car rental rates are lower. And inglenooks are less crowded.

YE OLDE BELL (1135 A.D.) This inn is the pride and joy of Hurley, on the Thames. Britain's most intriguing inns are pinpointed in "Inns of Britain," a free 56-page guide. See offer below.

For free 56-page booklet "The Inns of Britain," write, British Travel Association, Dept. 692 at 680 Fifth Ave., N.Y., N.Y. 10019; or 612 So. Flower St., Los Angeles, Calif. 90017; or 39 So. LaSalle St., Chicago, Ill. 69603; or 151 Bloor St. West, Toronto.

The main ingredient of Ogilvy's style was "image": that is, the construction of the advertisements in such a way that Great Britain was made to appear as the repository of everything civilized, majestic and awesome, yet retaining a bucolic charm unique among all the countries of the world. England was romantic yet familiar, different yet safe, and permeated with something that America had little of: history. "I think," says Field, "that David almost gave the advertising world the word 'image.'"

"There are three reasons why I could write this kind of advertisement," says Ogilvy. "First, I came from a family of scholars. I was a scholar myself. Second, I was a door-to-door salesman [after being expelled from Oxford, he sold refrigerators in Edinburgh]. And third, I was a research man [his research background led him to discover, for his British Travel Association ads, that readership would go up if he included a car in the picture—no matter what the picture was about]."

Perhaps the best reason for the campaign's success, and for the notable failure of its many imitators, was that Ogilvy and Field were writing about their own country. "This advertising," says Field, "is better done by an Englishman than an American." In 1950, before Ogilvy got the account, 90,000 Americans visited Britain, as compared with 110,000 who visited France. In 1967 839,000 visited Britain, while only 650,000 visited France. The advertising is likely to have had something to do with that.

Rolls-Royce

The most famous automobile ad ever written is reproduced in *Plate 61.* It was the first ad Ogilvy ever did for Rolls-Royce, and it was all he ever had to do. It ran once, in April, 1958, in *The New York Times,* *The New Yorker,* the *Wall Street Journal,* and *Sunset* magazine, at a total media and production cost of $25,000, and it sold $6 million worth of Rolls-Royces. Now $6 million worth of Rolls-Royces happens to be only three hundred cars,[1] which perhaps makes the story less dramatic, except that the Rolls-Royce factory could turn out only four hundred per year *in toto.* Since American sales had never exceeded one hundred cars annually, this necessitated a most drastic overhaul of factory and sales procedures, and that, ironically enough, was what finally led to Ogilvy's resigning the account.

In the meantime, however, dealers were ecstatic. One Chicago dealer sold $350,000 worth in a week. Back orders piled up, and there was soon an eighteen-month wait for delivery. The factory went on a round-the-clock basis, increased its capacity as well as it could, and tried to reschedule its deliveries so that more cars could be shipped to the United States.

While the buyers waited, those who cared had ample time to reflect on

---

[1]An approximation, of course. Rolls-Royce cars range in price from $15,000 to $30,000.

"At 60 miles an hour the loudest noise in this new Rolls-Royce comes from the electric clock"

What _makes_ Rolls-Royce the best car in the world? "There is really no magic about it—
it is merely patient attention to detail," says an eminent Rolls-Royce engineer.

1. "At 60 miles an hour the loudest noise comes from the electric clock," reports the Technical Editor of THE MOTOR. The silence of the engine is uncanny. Three mufflers tune out sound frequencies — acoustically.

2. Every Rolls-Royce engine is run for seven hours at full throttle before installation, and each car is test-driven for hundreds of miles over varying road surfaces.

3. The Rolls-Royce is designed as an *owner-driven* car. It is eighteen inches shorter than the largest domestic cars.

4. The car has power steering, power brakes and automatic gear-shift. It is very easy to drive and to park. No chauffeur required.

5. There is no metal-to-metal contact between the body of the car and the chassis frame—except for the speedometer drive. The entire body is insulated and under-sealed.

6. The finished car spends a week in the final test-shop, being fine-tuned. Here it is subjected to ninety-eight separate ordeals. For example, the engineers use a *stethoscope* to listen for axle-whine.

7. The Rolls-Royce is guaranteed for *three years*. With a new network of dealers and parts-depots from Coast to Coast, service is no longer any problem.

8. The famous Rolls-Royce radiator has never been changed, except that when Sir Henry Royce died in 1933 the monogram RR was changed from red to black.

9. The coachwork is given five coats of primer paint, and hand rubbed between each coat, before *fourteen* coats of finishing paint go on.

10. By moving a switch on the steering column, you can adjust the shock-absorbers to suit road conditions. (The lack of fatigue in driving this car is remarkable.)

11. Another switch defrosts the rear window, by heating a network of 1360 invisible wires in the glass. There are two separate ventilating systems, so that you can ride in comfort with all the windows closed. Air conditioning is optional.

12. The seats are upholstered with eight hides of English leather—enough to make 128 pairs of soft shoes.

13. A picnic table, veneered in French walnut, slides out from under the dash. Two more swing out behind the front seats.

14. You can get such optional extras as an Espresso coffee-making machine, a dictating machine, a bed, hot and cold water for washing, an electric razor.

15. You can lubricate the entire chassis by simply pushing a pedal from the driver's seat. A gauge on the dash shows the level of oil in the crankcase.

16. Gasoline consumption is remarkably low and there is no need to use premium gas; a happy economy.

17. There are two separate systems of power brakes, hydraulic and mechanical. The Rolls-Royce is a very *safe* car—and also a very *lively* car. It cruises serenely at eighty-five. Top speed is in excess of 100 m.p.h.

18. Rolls-Royce engineers make periodic visits to inspect owners' motor cars and advise on service.

ROLLS-ROYCE AND BENTLEY

19. The Bentley is made by Rolls-Royce. Except for the radiators, they are identical motor cars, manufactured by the same engineers in the same works. The Bentley costs $300 less, because its radiator is simpler to make. People who feel diffident about driving a Rolls-Royce can buy a Bentley.

PRICE. The car illustrated in this advertisement— f.o.b. principal port of entry—costs **$13,550.**

If you would like the rewarding experience of driving a Rolls-Royce or Bentley, get in touch with our dealer. His name is on the bottom of this page. Rolls-Royce Inc., 10 Rockefeller Plaza, New York, N. Y.

JET ENGINES AND THE FUTURE

Certain airlines have chosen Rolls-Royce turbo-jets for their Boeing 707's and Douglas DC8's. Rolls-Royce prop-jets are in the Vickers Viscount, the Fairchild F.27 and the Grumman Gulfstream.

Rolls-Royce engines power more than half the turbo-jet and prop-jet airliners supplied to or on order for world airlines.

Rolls-Royce now employ 42,000 people and the company's engineering experience does not stop at motor cars and jet engines. There are Rolls-Royce diesel and gasoline engines for many other applications.

The huge research and development resources of the company are now at work on many projects for the future, including nuclear and rocket propulsion.

Plate 61

the ad. The headline's claim was such a blatant challenge that one felt it *had* to be true. People on superhighways rolled up the windows of their American cars to see if they could even *hear* the electric clock, much less have it drown out the sound of everything else. Detroit car manufacturers felt the claim to be so strong that five years later, when Ogilvy no longer even had the account, Ford based an entire year's campaign on the claim that at sixty miles per hour the new Ford was quieter than a Rolls-Royce.

Interestingly enough, in 1933 Charles Brower of Batten, Barton, Durstine & Osborne had written an advertisement for Pierce-Arrow (a luxury car) that said: "*The only sound* one can hear in the new Pierce-Arrows is the ticking of the electric clock."[2] The difference between the two claims is instructive. Where Brower's claim was typical hyperbole of the era (the italics were his), and was demonstrably false on its face, Ogilvy's claim that the clock simply made the *loudest* noise was demonstrably true. It was not known, however, if Rolls-Royce was installing an exceptionally loud clock.

In the four years that Ogilvy had the Rolls-Royce account, the total number of ads he did was very small. They were designed to encourage Americans who had always thought of the car as a chauffeur-driven limousine to consider buying the smaller version and driving it themselves.

Though not as remarkable as the first, these later ads were all effective in signing up buyers—so effective, in fact, that Rolls-Royce, flooded with orders and unable to make deliveries, cut back its annual advertising budget in each of the four years in order not to sell too many cars. Unfortunately, even three hundred American sales per year were too many for the factory to make properly, and the car's quality deteriorated. It had been a Rolls-Royce tradition, and an important selling point, that the company would not deliver a car that was not perfect. But by 1962 hundreds of the newly purchased cars were found to be lemons, and Ogilvy was said to feel that he could no longer in good conscience advertise them.

It was also rumored that Ogilvy had heard he could get the Buick account for the agency, an account whose billings of $20 million per year were approximately two hundred times what he was getting from Rolls-Royce. In any case, he resigned the account in May of 1962, and it went to LaRoche, McCaffrey & McCall, the agency of his former copy chief David McCall.

If Ogilvy resigned Rolls-Royce to get Buick, he was disappointed. He did not get the account, and, in fact, has never had an American car

---

[2]There is little possibility of even unintentional plagiarism on Ogilvy's part, since the BBDO ad ran only once, in an American magazine *(House Beautiful),* years before Ogilvy ever set foot in this country.

account. Detroit advertising is notoriously mediocre, with the occasional exception of Ford (J. Walter Thompson), and until 1967 none of the so-called creative agencies like Ogilvy, Jack Tinker & Partners, or Doyle Dane Bernbach had ever handled an American car. That year, however, Wells, Rich, Greene got the American Motors account from Benton & Bowles, and began an aggressive, stylish campaign in a desperate attempt to keep the company from going bankrupt. Wells, Rich, Greene's style—a more flamboyant version of Carl Ally's—had made the agency one of the greatest successes in the history of advertising. By its very flamboyance, it is likely to have the effect of making Ogilvy more acceptable to the Detroit "Big Three" (General Motors, Ford and Chrysler), and it may not be long before Ogilvy gets the American car account he has always wanted.

Puerto Rico

As anyone past high school age is aware, Puerto Rico was America's first colony, the United States having annexed it as part of its Spanish-American War booty; and for the next fifty years it was raped, exploited and forgotten. Ruled by absentee sugar plantation and rum distillery owners, the island existed on a subsistence level until World War II. But because of its rum, the war gave Puerto Rico the means to escape its colonial status.

During the war, American drinkers couldn't get Scotch, and most domestic grain was being used for food instead of liquor. But Puerto Rico's sugar was still largely available to local distillers, and they began shipping to the mainland all the rum they could make. It was "green," unaged, barely legal rotgut liquor, but it was all there was. The government of Puerto Rico, collecting a tax on every gallon, had by the end of the war accumulated over $60 million in rum taxes, and under the direction of the extraordinary Governor Luis Muñoz Marín began to spend it on his famous Operation Bootstrap. Teachers were sent to every village, and villagers were paid by the government to build them schoolhouses to teach in. Agricultural experts taught good crop management, and land reform forced a breakaway from a one-crop economy. Houses were designed that could be built by those who would live in them, with the cost of materials subsidized by the government, and with wages paid to the builders for their work. Experts in many fields came from all over the world to help out, and a number of other underdeveloped countries sent delegations to learn from the Puerto

After office hours in Puerto Rico. Photograph by Elliott Erwitt.

The Executive Life in Puerto Rico

THE OTHER DAY somebody questioned our wisdom in stressing the good life in Puerto Rico. "If life is so delightful," he said, "how can you expect executives to *work?*"

Well, they do. Over four hundred and fifty U. S. manufacturers have set up new plants on this sunny island. *Their net profit on sales is three times as high as the average in the United States.*

These figures speak volumes. They reflect the stimulus of Puerto Rico's remarkable Operation Bootstrap. They also give some idea of the extraordinary industrial renaissance that is attracting manufacturers at the rate of *three new plants a week.*

But they cannot express the more personal rewards you get from being part of it all. Hence our picture. It was taken on Luquillo Beach. After a hard day, wouldn't *you* appreciate a sea so warmly gentle it doesn't even tickle the soles of your feet? And how about a house in those green hills?

It's all within the bounds of possibility. This whole idyllic picture is under five and a half hours from New York.

©1958 – Commonwealth of Puerto Rico, 666 Fifth Avenue, New York 19, N. Y.

Plate 62

Plate 63

**A new day is dawning
in Puerto Rico**

IT IS DAWN. A gentle trade wind silks across the Condado Lagoon. And from beyond the Caribe Hilton comes the muffled boom of surf.

Our photograph has a serenity that we hope you will feel as soon as you set foot in Puerto Rico. For here is an island that can show you progress and beauty walking hand-in-hand.

You land at Isla Verde, a brilliantly modern airport.

It cost sixteen million dollars—but it has a soul. As your bags are unloaded, someone hands you a frozen daiquiri—complimentary of course. Nobody asks you for a passport. You walk straight to your taxi, past lily ponds and fountains.

On the road to your hotel, you see modern homes that make a northern life seem stuffy and Victorian. Sun-dappled Spanish patios, flowering hibiscus and

a disarming friendliness of open doors and windows. The climate comes right in because there is nothing unpleasant to keep out.

You begin to realize why so many U.S. companies are starting new operations in Puerto Rico. With Operation Bootstrap's irresistible incentives to new industry, the whole proposition makes sense. A serene place to live. An exciting place to work.

®1959—Commonwealth of Puerto Rico, 666 Fifth Ave., N.Y.

Ricans. Those who were there at the time recall the incredible spirit that suffused the entire country. Years later, when John F. Kennedy established the Peace Corps and the Alliance for Progress, he never sufficiently acknowledged his debt to Muñoz and his own corps.

In the first few years of Operation Bootstrap enormous strides were made, but by the early 1950s the money was running out. Wartime rum had been so bad in quality that as soon as other whiskeys became available again in the States, Americans stopped drinking the rum. As sales dropped, so did tax revenues, and with them the money available to finance the island's revolution. The government set up quality-improvement laws and research facilities for the distillers, and then decided to promote its rums by advertising in the United States.

This in itself was an unusual idea, comparable, for instance, to the state of Kentucky advertising its bourbons to the rest of the country. The mainland's concept of government's role in commercial or economic life—and in promoting the welfare of its citizens—is quite different from Puerto Rico's.

Muñoz appointed Teodoro Moscoso (who was later to become director of the Alliance for Progress) to run the Commonwealth's advertising and promotion program for rum and tourism, in the United States. On the

Plate 64

Girl by a gate
—in old San Juan

TIME STANDS STILL in this Puerto Rican patio. That weathered escutcheon bears the Royal Arms of Spain. You might have stepped back three centuries. In a sense, you have.

You start to wonder. Can this really be the Puerto Rico everybody is talking about? Is this the island where American industry is now expanding at the rate of three new plants a week? Is this truly the scene of a twentieth-century renaissance? Ask any proud Puerto Rican. He will surely answer—yes.

Within minutes from this patio, you will see the signs. Some are spectacular. The new hotels, the four-lane highways, the landscaped apartments. And some are down-to-earth. A tractor in a field, a village clinic, a shop that sells refrigerators. Note all these things. But, above all, *meet the people.*

Renaissance has a way of breeding remarkable men. Men of industry who can also love poetry. Men of courage who can also be tender. Men of vision who can also respect the past. Make a point of talking to these twentieth-century Puerto Ricans.

It won't be long before you appreciate the deeper significance of Puerto Rico's renaissance. You'll begin to understand why men like Pablo Casals and Juan Ramón Jiménez (the Nobel Prize poet) have gone there to live.

© 1958—Commonwealth of Puerto Rico,
666 Fifth Avenue, New York 19, N. Y.

◀ *How to find this patio in old San Juan. Ask for the City Hall. They call it the Ayuntamiento, in Spanish. Walk straight through this 17th Century building and there is your patio. Our photograph was taken by Elliott Erwitt.*

CASALS TENTH

A time for rejoicing in Puerto Rico

WHEN Pablo Casals steps up to the podium on June 1st, he will be conducting more than just the opening concert of just another music festival.

The Festival Casals is celebrating its tenth birthday in San Juan. Once again Don Pablo will conduct and play.

His friends will come from all over the globe to take part in his Festival: Artur Rubinstein, Igor Oistrakh, Leopold Simoneau, Justino Diaz, Mieczyslaw Horszowski, Alexander Schneider, Eugene Ormandy, and others.

But there will be another reason to celebrate in this sunny Commonwealth.

Over the past ten years, Pablo Casals and his Festival have sparked off a cultural *renaissance*. Next month's Festival Casals is one of its highlights. Another month it may be classical theatre in an old Spanish fortress. Or an art gallery opening in Old San Juan. Or ballet, or opera, or a festival of international drama.

High in a mountain village of Puerto Rico a symphony orchestra may be playing Mozart in a shady town plaza. Or a troupe of actors playing Molière, Cervantes or Shakespeare.

Come to Puerto Rico and share the island's enthusiasm for music and painting, dance and drama. You will appreciate why Pablo Casals came to live here.

And why he says "each day in Puerto Rico I am reborn."

Commonwealth of Puerto Rico, 666 Fifth Avenue, New York 10019

Plate 65

recommendation of his public relations agency, Moscoso contacted Ogilvy and asked his opinion of the advertising then being done ("7 nights, 6 days, for just $59.95"). "Well, that's quite nice," Ogilvy commented, "but why would anyone want to go there? It's no use your advertising for American tourists, because Americans think Puerto Rico is dirty, poor, disease-ridden, and has no beaches. It's no use advertising for American business, because American businessmen won't build factories there. What you must do is change the image of the country in American eyes."

This was not pure intuition on Ogilvy's part. When he had first heard of Moscoso's interest in the agency, he ordered a research survey of American attitudes toward Puerto Rico, and what he told Moscoso was exactly what the survey had told him: Puerto Rico was considered by Americans to be the "poorhouse of the Caribbean." When asked how they would rate certain tropical islands for such things as "beautiful beaches," for example, Hawaii came out first and Puerto Rico last. For "cleanliness," Puerto Rico was also last, as it was for "industrial progress," "modernity," "education," and "general attractiveness."

And in many ways they were right; having drained the country of everything profitable, Americans now looked down their noses at their handiwork. The island's per capita income in 1950 was $279, and its unemployment rate that year was 30 per cent. By 1955, in spite of impressive economic gains, more than half a million Puerto Ricans, out of a population of 2 million, had migrated to the mainland in search of work. Mainland Americans knew all this, and whatever opportunities Puerto Rico might have offered for new industries, and whatever attractions it might have had for tourists, were undercut by the attitudes of the very people who would have to invest in, or visit, the island.

In January of 1954, Moscoso hired Ogilvy to do the advertising for Puerto Rican rums, and in June of that year he added a separate budget for the Commonwealth itself, including tourism and new-industry programs.

Ogilvy's program was simply to advertise Puerto Rico as though, instead of finishing last in the survey, it had finished first. Gorgeous color photos of palm-fringed beaches, beautiful mountains, old Spanish courtyards in the heart of San Juan, Pablo Casals walking on the beach — most of the ads with white American couples enjoying themselves in apparent safety and comfort, to say nothing of pleasure — appeared month after month in *Holiday* and *The New Yorker (Plates 62–65).*

At the same time he began a campaign aimed at getting American businesses to build factories on the island. One ad in the series he considers to be the most effective of his entire career *(Plate 66).* The ad ran once, in *The New York Times,* the New York *Herald Tribune,* and *Fortune,* in January, 1955. It got three thousand qualified responses from American manufacturers, of whom sixty-four actually began construction of Puerto

Plate 66

Rican plants by the end of that year. The ad brought thousands of jobs, and millions of dollars of income, to the island. In all, about a thousand manufacturing plants have been built in Puerto Rico as a result of Operation Bootstrap, largely in the textile and electronics industries. The island's tourism has grown from 145,000 visitors in the 1955–56 season to more than 600,000 visitors in 1968-69. Rum tax revenues are back up to $60 million a year. More importantly, per capita income had risen to $1,037 by 1967, and unemployment had dropped to 12.6 per cent in the face of one of the highest birth rates in the world.

"Moscoso is the most remarkable man I have ever met in my advertising career," says Ogilvy. "He created the Casals Festival. He built the Caribe Hotel as part of Operation Bootstrap, so that tourists would have a modern hotel to stay in, then got Hilton to come in and manage it. He persuaded Laurance Rockefeller to build the Dorado Beach golf resort. He is responsible, as much as any man, for the rebirth of that country.

"Working on the Puerto Rico account is the greatest satisfaction I have had in my advertising career. I enjoy advertising on behalf of corporations, and it has been quite rewarding for me. But helping to rescue a country from starvation, and disease, and hopelessness — that was my greatest satisfaction."

4

The Campaign
of the Century

ALMOST EVERYONE IN THE advertising business has his own list of favorite advertising campaigns. Annual contests are held and awards given out by everyone from art directors to billboard salesmen. From year to year tastes change, new looks are recognized, and old looks forgotten. The best campaigns stop winning awards because they won everything in their first year or two, and no one wants to be so passé as to reward continued excellence. Agencies no longer believe Rosser Reeves' old claim that "I will let you have a brilliant campaign every six months — provided you change it every six months — and I'll take a less-than-brilliant campaign and beat your tail off with it because I'll run it ten years." But since 1949, when the first Ogilvy and Doyle Dane Bernbach ads appeared, there have been a few long-running campaigns that have stayed on most lists: Polaroid, Schweppes, Ohrbach's and Volkswagen are good examples.

Many people in the business, however, feel that Leo Burnett's advertising campaign for Marlboro cigarettes is the best single piece of sustained advertising work that has ever been done in this country. Helmut Krone, who created the Volkswagen and Avis campaigns, calls Marlboro "the campaign of the century." The initial insights that led to the creation of the product's image and how to sell it, back in the fall of 1954 when Burnett got the account, were so accurate that the first ad, which ran in a Dallas newspaper just to fill out an old schedule bought by the previous agency, could be run today with very few changes. Everything was there: the Marlboro man, the newly designed package, the completely masculine image that the cigarette projected (Plate 67). Almost every Marlboro advertisement and television commercial since then has been simply a repetition or enlargement or variation on that theme.

Although his Marlboro campaign has appeared on everybody's list for many years, Leo Burnett himself is a man who refuses to make lists. "If I had a favorite ad," he will tell you, "I wouldn't tell you." Burnett is the last of the old-time ad men. Born in Indiana in 1892, he has never worked farther east than Detroit. He founded his own agency in 1935, in Chicago rather than New York, where all his friends were going, out of an obstinate conviction that Chicago advertising could be as good as New York's. Although the agency is now the fifth largest in the country, and has six offices in the United States and Canada, he still insists that all creative work be done in Chicago, where he and his assistants can keep on top of it.

Burnett has recognized the fact that he is approaching eighty by cutting down on his working hours. He now works only ten hours a day, not including the commuting time from his farm, forty miles outside Chicago, which he moved to in order to cut down on his working time. He feels the move was worthwhile, however, because it means he spends fewer weekends working at the office.

Easterners find Burnett in person rather difficult to describe; he is nothing like a New York ad man, and you can pick any New York ad man you wish. He is medium short, medium portly, medium bald, and decidedly medium in flair, charm, gesture or other superficiality. "Spending an evening with Leo Burnett can be a horrendous experience," says one man who has known him for twenty years. "He has absolutely no small talk. All he knows is advertising."

Burnett is a copywriter by trade, and at his best he is not surpassed by Ogilvy or Bernbach. Most of his copy, however, is in the form of general essays on advertising, and memos to his staff on policy. It combines one of the world's homeliest philosophies with a killer instinct for the right phrase. When he founded the agency in 1935, he adopted the device of a hand reaching for the stars, which to this day appears on company stationery and brochures. Burnett said he had done it

. . . to express the inspiration and aspiration which we hoped to make the guiding spirit of our company. . . . When you "Reach for the Stars" you may not quite get one, but you won't get a handful of mud either. When you're constantly stretching up you're not likely to be looking down. When you're constantly trying for something better and higher you don't quite get conditioned to accepting something that's almost as good. . . . Anyway, if you're "Reaching for the Stars" you can't possibly get caught sitting on your *status quo.* It is suspected that *status quo* sitting is the prime cause of most cases of advertising arthritis.

Using the client's products, which to most agency people is a relic of advertising's sycophantic past, is no joke to Burnett. He smokes two packs of Marlboros a day, at least partly out of loyalty to his client. As he put it in a memo to the staff:

I guess my feeling is pretty well summed up in the remarks of the vice-president of a competitive agency. When asked why he was smoking a not-too-popular brand of cigarette which his company advertised, he replied: "In my book there is no taste or aroma quite like that of bread and butter."

P.S. Inasmuch as this memo expresses an entirely personal point of view, I can't resist adding that if any of us eats those nauseating Post Toasties or Wheaties, for example, in preference to the products of Kellogg's, I hope he chokes on them; and if any of us fertilizes his lawn without first trying Golden Vigoro, I hope it turns to a dark, repulsive brown.

Burnett may be footnoted by historians as the first flower-power businessman. On the day he opened the agency, he put a bowl of apples on the reception desk "just to brighten things up a bit, and as a sign of hospitality." Today there is a bowl of apples on every reception desk of every branch office of the agency, and they are eaten at the rate of 12,000 per year, which may make Burnett the largest single consumer of apples in the country. Burnett believes in apples. He also believes in good business practices: "We have three rules here regarding new accounts: (1) Is it a product to which advertising can contribute in terms of sales? (2) Are they good people to do business with? (3) Can they pay their bills? Life is too short to do business with sons of bitches."

Nor is he inarticulate about advertising. Reading his speeches (somewhat easier than listening to them, as he has no regard for the niceties of platform delivery and speaks at the pace, and with the inflections, of an electric typewriter), one finds an approach that underlies the best contemporary advertising:

"I have learned that people should be made to *want* your goods, not constantly induced to buy them.

"A lot of advertising apparently follows the rule that if you can't be smart, be big. What seems to be a 'hard-hitting' advertisement may be just loud and distracting. A turned page or tuned switch stops the noise.

"Don't try to *lure* people into reading your message. They know it's an ad and they like to look at good ads. Why try to fool them?"

Burnett's peculiar combination of instinct, Rotarian platitudes, and raw talent on wry has been the agency's biggest asset since the beginning. He invented the Green Giant for a small Minnesota vegetable packer, then twenty years later gave him a whole new life as the Jolly Green Giant. He kept the Santa Fe's passenger trains filled for years, even though its route was the longest and slowest to the Coast. His work for United Airlines, though hardly inspired, has helped to keep it in first place by far among United States airlines, and he has done the same for Kellogg cereals.

There is no question, however, that Marlboro is the work the agency grew famous on, and it came about this way. In 1954 there were six filter cigarettes already on the market: Winston, Kent, L & M, Viceroy, Tareyton and Parliament, in that order of sales. Together they shared 10 per cent of the market, which had not yet heard about lung cancer. (By 1970 filters had taken more than 75 per cent of the market, and the share is still rising.) Times were very bad indeed for Marlboro and its parent company Philip Morris. Marlboro was not a filter cigarette, although it came in a choice of ivory tip or red "beauty tip" to "keep the paper from your lips," and it was known as a woman's cigarette. Its share of market was less than one-quarter of one per cent, which in the cigarette business is quite near death. At the same time Philip Morris's total sales had been declining in the face of increases by its competitors.

The Marlboro agency was Cecil & Presbrey, a small company whose main distinction seems to have been that the account supervisor on Marlboro was the son of the chairman of the board of Philip Morris (the agency folded upon losing the account to Burnett).

In 1953 Philip Morris had hired Elmo Roper to do research on cigarette buying habits, in order to find out whether filters were really here to stay. Marlboro was to be the test subject, as it had the least to lose if the test should flop. Thousands of people were questioned about their emotional reactions to various brands, package colors, and filters. By May, 1954, while the account was still at Cecil & Presbrey, the new Marlboro, with a more aromatic blend of tobaccos, in its new red-white-and-black flip-top package, and its new filter, was put on sale as a test, in Dallas and Fort Worth. The package looked essentially as it does today, except that the top, which is now all red, was red-and-white striped.

Unfortunately the advertising was the same hollow sloganeering, and, although sales in Dallas went up, Cecil & Presbrey's stock at Philip Morris went down, and the company began looking for a new agency. Milton Biow, who had popularized the famous "Call for Philip Morris," and who was just then being finessed out of his agency by his own partners, put in a good word for Burnett, and in November, 1954, the account was officially transferred.

All the basic decisions on which Marlboro advertising has been built since the first Burnett ad appeared in January of 1955 were made at a meeting of the agency's top people that first November. David Ogilvy, speaking a few months after the campaign began, said, "I have no doubt that [Burnett's] judgment was illuminated by an intimate knowledge of consumer psychology with respect to cigarettes. But . . . before they started to create the advertising . . . they took some risks which few advertisers would take. Most notably, they seem to have decided that Marlboro should have an exclusively male personality. What a brave decision!"

Without question it was the right decision, and it would be said of most other advertising men that it was courageous. But somehow bravery is irrelevant to a discussion of Burnett. He is so unaware of alternatives and so uninvolved in the workings of his own mind that it would never occur to him to question his actions. When he speaks of his work, he admits to no uncertainties, and even the question of modesty or conceit is irrelevant. Advertising ideas speak through him the way Jesus speaks through Billy Graham. According to Burnett, the first meeting at the agency went like this:

"Our first job on the account was, they were in the middle of this

New from Philip Morris

Marlboro
FILTER CIGARETTES

NEW FLIP-TOP BOX

Firm to keep cigarettes from crushing. No tobacco in your pocket

Marlboro LONG SIZE

POPULAR FILTER PRICE

The new easy-drawing filter cigarette that delivers the goods on flavor. Long size. Popular filter price. Light up a Marlboro and be glad you've changed to a filter.

(MADE IN RICHMOND, VIRGINIA, FROM A NEW PHILIP MORRIS RECIPE)

Plate 67

The Marlboro Man

A lot of man . . . a lot of cigarette

"He gets a lot to like—filter, flavor, flip-top box." The works.
A filter that means business. An easy draw that's all
flavor. And the flip-top box that ends crushed cigarettes.

(MADE IN RICHMOND, VIRGINIA, FROM A PRIZED RECIPE)

NEW
"SELF-STARTER"
Just pull the tab
slowly and the
cigarettes pop
up. No digging.
No trouble.

POPULAR FILTER PRICE

Plate 68

test campaign in Dallas–Fort Worth, and we had to fill in the rest of the campaign just to make closing dates for the newspapers there. I said, 'I'll be damned if we'll do that; the first ad will be a *Burnett* ad.' We had this huddle with our top creative people—now this was all for this damn Dallas ad—and we thought, if filters were regarded on the sissy side, and Marlboro was regarded on the sissy side, the natural thing was to look for a masculine image. I asked around what was a masculine image and four or five people all said a cowboy. We dug out a picture of a cowboy from our art files and Lee Stanley [the art director] put it in big.

"We said this [the new cigarette] had to have a source, so we said, 'New from Philip Morris.' This had some status. People knew Philip Morris. We wanted to talk about flavor, too. What would a cowboy say about flavor?

"'Delivers the goods on flavor.'

"I had a background in foods, so I knew there had to be some source for this flavor. What about 'recipe'? So it was 'Made from a new Philip Morris recipe.'

"The package they were using seemed pink because of the stripes, and it had an effete look. Why not make it red? Take the damn stripes out of here.

"Well, we came to New York in December with one ad: the cowboy. They bought what we said, ripped the old package off the machines, and went with the ad *(Plate 67)*.

"But what were we going to do about the cowboy? Were we going to run the cowboy all our lives? So we looked for other men—men who were tough but they could eat at the Waldorf. I'll take credit for the tattoo—because we had run across this thing by Jack London: 'Follow any man with a tattoo and you will find a romantic and adventurous past.'[1]

"Well, we knew this photographer, Constantin Joffé, who was excellent at photographing non-professional models. So Joffé went down to this tattoo artist on the Brooklyn waterfront and got hold of his book of designs. And incidentally he had to pay $5,000 to the guy just to insure that he wouldn't lose the book, before the guy would *lend* it to him. So we started taking pictures of these guys with tattoos that we put on with ball-point pens. None of them were professionals, by the way. Our first model was a Navy lieutenant, another was Andy Armstrong, the agency's art supervisor. *(Plates 68, 69)*.

"Now, this was still all for the Dallas campaign, but then we ran it in New York and all over, and New York went crazy for it. Looking back

[1]Efforts to track down this line have been unsuccessful. In 1957 Leo Burnett wrote a three-page ad for *The New Yorker*, entitled *The Marlboro Story*, where he repeats the quotation but hedges it by saying, "... we ran across a remark attributed to Jack London. He is reported as saying, in effect, 'Follow. . . .'"

Plate 69

Marlboro

You get
a lot
to like

-filter
-flavor
-flip-top box

NEW
FLIP-TOP BOX

Sturdy to keep
cigarettes
from crushing.
No tobacco in
your pocket.
Up to date.

POPULAR
FILTER PRICE

Here's old-fashioned flavor in the new way to smoke. Man-size
taste of honest tobacco comes full through. Smooth-drawing filter feels
right in your mouth. Works fine but doesn't get in the way. Modern
Flip-Top Box keeps every cigarette firm and fresh until you smoke it.

(MADE IN RICHMOND, VIRGINIA, FROM A NEW MARLBORO RECIPE)

on it, it was the name, distinguished, probably associated with the Duke
of Marlboro, contrasted with the cowboy, and the flip-top package too,
well, it all added up. It spelled Mother."

Mother or not, a somewhat different story is told by Joffé. Though he
describes himself in a picturesque Russian-French accent as Burnett's

greatest fan, Joffé says, "The truth—the truth, not the legend, the truth—is the following: When I heard that Leo got the Marlboro account, I sent him a telegram that said CONGRATULATIONS. SUGGEST TO USE VIRILE BIG FACES OF MEN OF EVERYDAY OCCUPATIONS (forgive my bad English constructions).

"Leo called me up and asked me if we could talk about it. He brought his group and we talked in my conference room. Leo wanted a gimmick for these ads.

"'What is a manly gimmick?' he growls. You know, he growls, low. 'What is a rhmmm, rhmmm, rhmmm,' he says.

"My wife—not I but my wife, who was working for me at the time—suggested the tattoo. I was against it!

"Leo snapped at it: 'That's *good*, that's *good! Rhmmm rhmmm*, rhmmm *rhmmm!'*

"After he went back to Chicago, they came up with the idea of the cowboy. But we didn't use the tattoos until after the first ad.

"Did I pay $5,000 to a tattoo artist to borrow his book? Of course not. Well, we did go to a lot of tattoo artists, here in New York and in Philadelphia. Why Philadelphia? Because they had better artists there, down on the waterfront. We got many, many books of tattoo designs, from them, from libraries, books of Japanese and Indian tattoos. We were trying to find out what was really fashionable today in tattoos."

But Burnett disregarded the research and the suggestions of Joffé, and ordered him to use a simple military insignia.

"And that is Leo's genius!" says Joffé. "He simplifies, simplifies, until every extraneous thing has been removed."

The tattoo book that was finally used for most of the Marlboro shots was a piece discovered in a *National Geographic* from 1944. It was a collection of armed forces unit emblems from World War II. Lee Stanley, the art director on the account, would ink them on the models, and then spray them with Krylon, a fixative, for the shot.

"Leo is so smart about these things," says Joffé. "He wanted us to give a violent juxtaposition between the model and the occupation he would be photographed in. We would take a garage mechanic and make him a philosopher, you know, put him in a library with books, books all around.

"But overall, most of the most successful Marlboro men were pilots, and do you know why? Because pilots seem to have a little wrinkle around the eyes."

At any rate, Burnett was right about New York's going crazy for it. Even today, Marlboros outsell Winstons in New York—although nationwide, Winstons outsell Marlboros by two to one—and this was possibly Burnett's greatest satisfaction. His agency was then twenty years old and it still had a second-city complex; the Marlboro campaign meant it would be

Plate 70

130

1. (Music)

2. (Music under, Anncr VO) Marlboro--the filter cigarette with the unfiltered taste--takes you to the Los Angeles Coliseum.

3. It was here that this man set a Rams record that held for 14 years.

4. Meet Tom Harmon.

5. Settle back, Tom, with your Marlboro.

6. November 23, 1947. The Rams against the Lions. Remember?

7. You've got the ball and there you go--heading up field...

8. ...racing 88-yards on this punt return...

9. ... for a Rams record.

10. Well, Tom--you've been around football for a long time now.

11. HARMON: That's right. And one of the nicest parts has been my long association with Marlboro.

12. (Anncr VO) Glad to see you're a Marlboro man.

13. HARMON: Well, like the song says, you get a lot to like.

14. (Anncr VO) Marlboro's got the combination--lots of flavor and the selectrate filter.

15. Marlboro, the filter cigarette with the unfiltered taste.

taken seriously in New York. David Ogilvy called it ". . . a triumph of image-building. Virility without vulgarity, quality without snobbery. Already [after one year of the campaign] Marlboro has acquired a vivid personality in a chaotic field—and sales are great."

James D. Woolf, who was a columnist in *Advertising Age* at the time, also wrote about the campaign, taking as his theme a line from a nineteenth-century divine, Samuel Crothers: "'. . . every man is really two men:

the man he is and the man he wants to be.' It is to this 'man we want to be'—to the fictions we create about ourselves—that advertising can be made to appeal with special force." Woolf cited Marlboro as the best example of this type of advertising.

Owen Smith, a Leo Burnett vice-president and account supervisor on Marlboro since the start, calls the cowboy "an almost universal symbol of admired masculinity. . . . Women often tend to buy what they consider a

1. (Music)...

2. ...

3. ...

4. ...

5. ...

6. ...

7. ...

8. ...

9. ...

10. ...

11. ...

12. ...

13. ...

14. (Music under, Anncr VO)
Come to where the flavor is.

15. Come to Marlboro Country!
(Musical playoff.)

Plate 71

man's cigarette. So we show Marlboro being smoked by men who have been carefully selected to appeal to both sexes." The tattoo on the models, he says, suggests "a romantic past. We have never called undue attention to it in the advertising except to indicate to the reader that here is a man who came up the hard way and who is enjoying the fruits of his labor. . . .

132

Plate 72

You get a lot to like with a Marlboro—filter, flavor, pack or box.

Come to where the flavor is. Come to Marlboro Country.

Plate 73

We have followed the same pattern, the same format, since the first ad." The tattoo has disappeared from the ads in recent years, but it had long since made its point. Most people, in fact, still believe it is there.

The first ad appeared in January, 1955, and the budget for that year was $3.5 million. Sales jumped from near zero in 1954 to 6.4 billion cigarettes. In 1956 Marlboro sold 14.3 billion, and in 1957 19.5 billion. "Then, in 1958," says Smith, "the *Reader's Digest* thing hit us." The *Reader's Digest* thing, it may be recalled, was the first public documentation of just how bad cigarettes are for you, and how ineffective most filters are in removing cancer-causing agents. Only Kent, the *Digest* said, had a worthwhile filter. The other brands were laid out in varying degrees of malevolence for all to behold and switch from. For the next two years Marlboro sales stayed exactly where they were in 1957 while Kent sales more than doubled, to take over second place among filters behind the undisputed leader, Winston.

Winston, by the way, was introduced a year before Marlboro by R. J. Reynolds, a company four times as large as Philip Morris, with three times as many salesmen available to push it, and an introductory advertising budget of over $15 million. The cigarette got national distribution immediately, something Marlboro finally achieved in 1960, and has always held a large sales lead over its competitors. Its bad-grammar advertising campaign, which was praised for its colloquialism and damned for perverting the language, may ultimately be found to have been irrelevant to its success.

"The *Digest* scare," as it is referred to in the trade, produced a series of commercials in which Julie London seduced Marlboro Men by singing "Where there's a man, there's a Marlboro" in their ears. "Christ," says Owen Smith, "we tried *everything*."

Ultimately they went back to Marlboro Men, alone, in masculine situations. Smith had, in 1956, bought television sponsorship of the National Football League for Marlboro, and it remained a staple of the advertising budget for twelve years. In 1960 Burnett produced a series of commercials featuring old football heroes, with newsreel footage of their great moments *(Plate 70)*.

Then, in 1962, the agency purchased the rights to Elmer Bernstein's score for the motion picture *The Magnificent Seven,* for an amount "too high to talk about," according to Burnett. To go with the music, the agency ("We have absolutely no pride of authorship here," says Burnett. "Nobody knows for sure who produced which of our ads.") created the phrase "Marlboro Country," and returned to a western theme, but allowed greater freedom in cinematography and editing to its commercial filmmakers. The result was one of the most beautifully photographed series of television commercials and print ads ever done in this country *(Plates 71–73)*.

At any rate Marlboro sales, which were held back again from 1962 through 1964 because of the "Surgeon-General's scare," rose again through 1969, and in 1967 the brand overtook Kent for second place among filters, behind Winston.

The end, of course, is in sight, as it is for all cigarette advertising (see final chapter). Burnett and his fellow cigarette salesmen will have to bear their share of the guilt for creating a generation of addicts, many of whom are now condemned to death from lung cancer. But there is an innocence to Burnett, a childlike pleasure in his craft, that survives moral attack.

"If you have found anything of value," a speech of his once concluded, "in this compost heap of experiences and observations, you are mightily welcome to it. My parting word of advice is to steep yourself in your subject, work like hell, and love, honor, and obey your hunches."

5

Two Great Campaigns From Stoop, Prone & Bending, Inc.

ANYONE IN THE AGENCY business is likely to know that Foote, Cone &
Belding, Inc., with billings of more than $300 million in 1969, is the
sixth largest advertising agency in the world. And *since* he is in the agency
business, he will be hard put to understand why, since most of its work
is mediocre, it lacks a driving personality at the top, and it allows its
clients to change or veto advertisements almost at will. "You must give
the client at least two campaigns to choose from; if you just bring him
one campaign, he'll think you didn't work hard enough," says Fairfax
M. Cone, head of the agency.

This attitude has tended to attract docile, gelded Mad-Ave types to
FCB, the security-minded androgynes of this malevolently sexual business,
who would rather submit than fight a client bent on raping a campaign.
What was once the most creative, assertive agency in the country—when
it was Lord & Thomas, and Albert Lasker and Claude Hopkins ran it—has
taken refuge from originality in a cocoon of research devices, and now
can do its best work only on those infrequent occasions when the clients
themselves encourage imagination.

When they do, however, the results can be very good indeed, for in the
middle of the wasteland two superb campaigns were created. Both of
them found a compelling idea to start with, both had the taste to stay
with it for years, refining and improving it, and both were extraordinarily
successful in selling their products. The first campaign is for Contac cold
pills, and the second is for Clairol hair colorings, which William Bernbach
has called his favorite in the business. Bernbach's comment is interesting
not simply because he has a good claim to being the best advertising man
in the United States, but because he regards good advertising as an end
in itself, and appreciates most those in the business who make good ads.
Foote, Cone & Belding does not agree, regarding itself as a marketing arm
of the client, which only incidentally makes advertisements. It is the rare
marketing arm, however, that has enough creative freedom to make
good advertisements, and over the years Doyle Dane Bernbach has done
incomparably better work.

On occasion, however, and perhaps just through fortunate accident,
FCB has been able to bring together creative ad-makers, account executives
with taste, and clients with courage enough to trust them, and then
produce good advertising.

Contac

In the world of patent medicines (or proprietary drugs, if you will—and you will if the pharmaceutical houses have their way) the search never ends for that one great cold pill that *everybody* will want to take. In the late 1950s Dristan dominated the market, with high-powered, sock-it-to-'em commercials. It had developed the Nasograph, which measured clogged nostrils with an accuracy never before achieved on television. By 1959 Dristan was spending over $13 million per year in advertising, to reach a market whose total sales that year for all cold remedies combined was $65 million. This is in line with common practice in the drug business (about 50 per cent of retail sales are put into advertising), and is quite revealing of just how much—or little—the consumer gets for his money.

(One of the few exceptions to this rule has been Coricidin, the intellectual's cold pill, which is advertised only to doctors and druggists. Your doctor was meant to turn you on to it himself by giving you his free samples. After that you were free to switch, if you dared defy him. Coricidin has always been the most profitable of the cold pills, because its advertising cost is such a low percentage of its sales.)

In 1959, when Smith, Kline & French, an old, established ethical (prescriptions only) drug company decided to enter the cold-pill business, it had the imagination not to copy what was already being sold, but to gamble on an entirely new approach for proprietary drugs: the spansule, or "tiny time pill" concept of medication. In addition, SKF created a new company just to market the product, named the company Menly & James Laboratories (Menly & James was a defunct English corporation whose name SKF had bought a few years earlier because it sounded so respectable), and made its own advertising manager president of the company.

Peter Godfrey, the new president, selected Foote, Cone & Belding because he wanted marketing and design assistance, as well as advertising, from his agency. FCB was to choose the product's name, design the package, and prepare the advertising. Godfrey stipulated only that distribution had to be through druggists and drug wholesalers, who were not likely to sell the product at a discount, as food chains were discounting Dristan and costing druggists sales. "We were riding SKF's coattails with this product," says Godfrey, "and we couldn't afford to compromise the parent company's reputation with druggists."

Two art directors at the agency designed the flat cardboard package —large, simple, clean, with a pill visible through a cellophane window, a radical departure from the dark bottles of the competition; hard *not* to

Here comes Daddy with a cold for everybody.

A few sneezes here and there and suddenly your whole family could be sharing Daddy's cold. Which is good reason for keeping Contac® on hand. Because a single Contac capsule works fast to help check your sneezes, stop your sniffles, and clear your stuffy nose. And the 600 tiny "time pills" inside keep on working up to 12 hours.

You get gentle relief all day or all night from the good medicine in just one Contac capsule. And when you're not sneezing and sniffling and blowing, you're not spreading as many cold germs. And you'll be a family hero for that. Get Contac at your pharmacy.

Plate 74

buy if you were looking for cold pills, and easy to make a big counter display with. A copywriter thought up the name Dynate for the product (day-night, get it?), and things were ready to roll in the fall of 1960, as soon as approval was received from the Food and Drug Administration.

But government approval did not come until the summer of 1961, and during that year many changes were made in the advertising. "That year's delay was the best thing that could have happened to the product," says Jack Avrett, who was then the copywriter on the account, and is now an associate creative director at Wells, Rich, Greene. "It gave us a chance to refine our thinking and do a lot of experimental work. And it was easier to do it with this company because they didn't have masses of product managers to go through; here there were only two men to deal with in the whole company."

One of the first things changed was the name. Dynate was not legally available for the product, and Contac ("continuous action") was chosen instead.

The crucial element of the advertising, it was felt, was the visualization of the "tiny time pills"—the hundreds of little pills that were coated so as to dissolve in the intestine at various rates, releasing decongestants, antihistamines and the like over a twelve-hour period. Raymond Betuel, then the account's art director and now head of the New York office's art department, says: "We had to demonstrate how this product worked, but how to show it was where everybody had his own idea. A lot of guys wanted animation. It was my idea to use photomicrography. When I said it, I didn't know how it could be done, but I figured there must be some guy in New York who could do it. I met this photographer, Norman Gaines, who loved photographing the heads of pins, and we shot a hell of a lot of experimental footage. We finally dropped the pills through liquid in front of the lens, and that became the key shot in all the commercials." The phrase "tiny time pills" was itself a revision of an earlier copy line, which read "pellets of cold-releasing medication."

All the changes, though, were in line with the first decision that Godfrey had made, which was to fly in the face of the Dristan ads and use a "pleasant sell." This is a mood that Contac advertising has managed to keep over the years (Plates 74–78).

Test marketing was set to begin in the fall of 1961. Someone had heard a rumor, however, that a competitive product was coming out then, and so it was decided to forget about testing and go national right away. SKF had good distribution with drug wholesalers all over the country, and, by promising not to distribute through food chains and discounters, Contac got good store position and big displays. Since 75 per cent of the cold-remedy market is in drug stores, the decision did not cost SKF much business; and, since some drug wholesalers sell to food stores as well,

Get ahead
of your cold

before it
gets ahold of
your head.

The sooner you treat your cold to Contac® the better.

Because over 600 "tiny time pills" in each capsule can help protect you against trouble-making sniffles. Can keep your nose un-stuffy for up to 12 hours. And can head your sneezes off (before you sneeze your head off).

Just two Contac capsules a day. One in the morning. Another at night. That's all it takes to keep you ahead of every cold you catch.

At your pharmacy. From Menley & James Laboratories, Philadelphia.

Plate 75

even that market loss was negligible. Contac went on the market in September, 1961, and within three weeks was being sold in 90 per cent of all American drugstores.

Most of the advertising budget was, and is still, in television. For the introduction, however, FCB ordered a four-page, booklet-type advertisement in the *Reader's Digest,* at a cost of about $200,000. But when the issue appeared, it seemed the *Digest* had placed the pages incorrectly — a sin

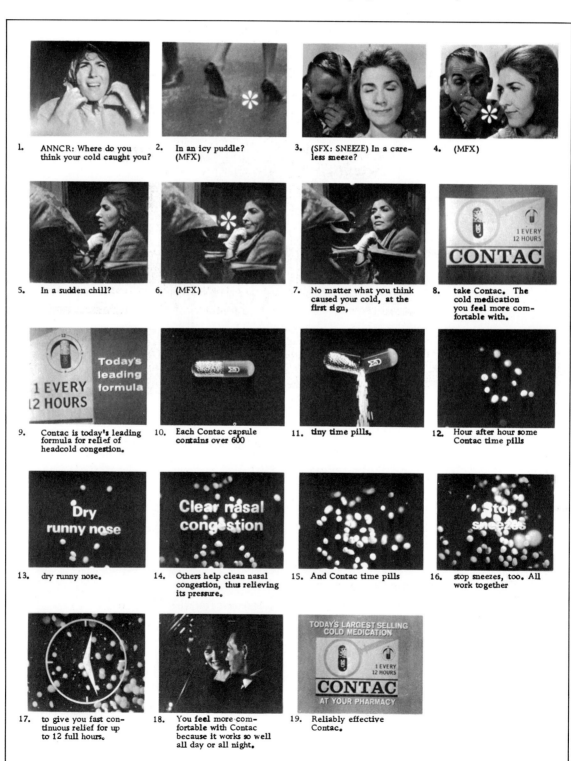

1. ANNCR: Where do you think your cold caught you?

2. In an icy puddle? (MFX)

3. (SFX: SNEEZE) In a careless sneeze?

4. (MFX)

5. In a sudden chill?

6. (MFX)

7. No matter what you think caused your cold, at the first sign,

8. take Contac. The cold medication you **feel** more comfortable with.

9. Contac is today's leading formula for relief of headcold congestion.

10. Each Contac capsule contains over 600

11. tiny time pills.

12. Hour after hour some Contac time pills

13. dry runny nose.

14. Others help clean nasal congestion, thus relieving its pressure.

15. And Contac time pills

16. stop sneezes, too. All work together

17. to give you fast continuous relief for up to 12 full hours.

18. You **feel** more comfortable with Contac because it works so well all day or all night.

19. Reliably effective Contac.

Plate 76

144

Plate 77

145

Help stamp out runny noses.

Just one Contac® capsule works up to twelve hours
to relieve sniffles, sneezes and stuffy nose.
Contac is today's largest-selling cold medication
at your pharmacy.

1 EVERY
12 HOURS

CONTAC

MENLEY & JAMES LABORATORIES, Philadelphia, Pa.
Proprietary Pharmaceuticals made to Ethical Standards

in the agency business comparable to, say, Spiro Agnew shouting "Off the pigs!" at a White House reception.

Naturally the *Digest* agreed to run the four-page ad again, in its next issue, with the pages correctly placed, at no charge. The practice is called a "make-good," and it made an excellent effect on Contac's initial sales. Within eighteen months Contac was not only the largest-selling cold remedy in the country, but the largest-selling brand of proprietary drug sold in all drugstores. By 1967 it had reached a yearly volume of about

That's a promising cold you've got there.
With a little neglect

it
can
be
a
honey

Why give up and give in to a cold? Go to work on it early. Take Contac® when you *first* feel your cold coming on.

Right away, over 600 tiny "time pills" in each Contac capsule will begin stopping your sniffles. Checking your sneezes. Clearing your stuffy nose. You may never even feel the worst part of your cold.

And the good medicine in Contac keeps up its good work continuously—for up to 12 full hours.

Instead of giving your next cold nothing but neglect, why not give it everything we've got?

Get Contac at your pharmacy. And take it early. Before your cold gets worse.

CONTAC

Menley & James Laboratories,
Philadelphia

Plate 78

$30 million in a total market of $120 million, of which it spent about $15 million with Foote, Cone & Belding for advertising.

In early 1969 the agency did a very bizarre thing, probably attributable to an overwhelming desire to outproduce Mary Wells of Wells, Rich, Greene. It made a television commercial for Contac called "Cold Diggers of 1969," a parody of a Busby Berkeley musical number. The commercial featured lines of girls singing and tapping their way through a choreographed reproduction of the sinus passages, with an illuminated sign behind them flashing thousands of bulbs in perfect synchronization, animating the action of the pills. It was totally charming, quite sophisticated, well directed and produced, and would not have moved three boxes of Contac across the counter in a penny sale. It also cost $250,000 to make.

The commercial won awards at various advertising competitions all during the spring of 1969, but in June Menly & James took the account away from FCB and gave it to Ogilvy & Mather.

Moral: To thine own self be true.

Clairol

"'Does she . . . or doesn't she?' When I was a high school girl in Brooklyn, that meant does she or doesn't she neck, which in those days was going pretty far. When I wrote that line for Clairol, of course I was aware of the double meaning. But the line is about hair coloring: 'Hair color so natural, only her hairdresser knows for sure.' When you write a line like that, that has more than one meaning, the prime meaning must be what you are really saying. People must feel that *you* didn't get the double meaning, that only *they* got it."

Shirley Polykoff, who wrote the line, may be America's first psychoanalyzed Jewish grandmother (she has been known to tell aspiring copywriters not to spend their money on "higher" education but to put it into analysis instead). She may also be one of the few people ever to take a common double-entendre and turn it into a respectable phrase. Miss Polykoff (she is a widow but has always used her maiden name in business) is a vice-president and copy chief at Foote, Cone & Belding, where she has written all Clairol advertising since the agency got the account in 1955.

At that time, Clairol was a small company in a small business. Most hair coloring was done in beauty parlors, and, in Miss Polykoff's words, "Only fast women and divorcées would use hair coloring." Only 7 per cent of American women had ever tried to color their hair, and the

Plate 79

148

Does she...or doesn't she?

Hair color so natural only her hairdresser knows for sure!

That beautiful feeling of belonging . . . his serene acceptance that *she's* the *prettiest mommy in the whole world.* Naturally, she treasures this feeling and manages *always* to look radiant . . . to keep her hair lively with sparkling color. It's *so* easy. And Miss Clairol *takes only minutes!* So *she'll never let gray* or *faded hair* age her looks. Not when it's so rewarding to stay young for one's self and one's family!

With Miss Clairol, finished tone is soft, ladylike . . . fresh, natural-looking in *any* light. That's why most hairdressers recommend Miss Clairol use it *every* time to add *young* color to fading hair . . . and to hide gray. With results so sure, *why wait* to look younger, more attractive? Try Miss Clairol yourself. *Today.* In wonderful new Creme Formula or Regular.

MISS CLAIROL HAIR COLOR BATH·

© 1957 Clairol Incorporated, Stamford, Conn. Available also in Canada

MORE WOMEN USE MISS CLAIROL THAN ANY OTHER HAIR COLORING

business was almost exclusively in the hands of hairdressers. What advertising there was was banal, was aimed at the hairdresser himself, and generally featured nothing but bright reds, oranges and blues. It is understandable that few women tried it.

Clairol's advertising budget for the first year was to be $400,000. Miss Polykoff wrote three alternative advertisements to be submitted to the client. This was in keeping with FCB's policy of letting the client determine what his advertising should be. One was the famous "Does

she . . . or doesn't she?" The second was "Tear up those baby pictures
. . . I'm a redhead now!" Miss Polykoff has forgotten what the third one
was, but says that she wrote the second two only in order to sell "Does
she . . .," which shows how to beat the system if you really want to.

When she showed the advertisement to the FCB directors she was not
taken seriously. "The men said, 'Honey, you must be kidding. You'll
never get away with that,'" Miss Polykoff later reported. "I said, 'The
dirt's in your own mind, boys,' and acted innocent. The ad simply asks

Is it true...
blondes
have more
fun?

Just be a blonde and see—a Lady Clairol blonde with silky, shining hair. Suddenly you'll know why skiing's smooth for blondes. Snow is snowier for blondes. Men adore you, do more for you, life is glowy-ier for blondes. So switch to bewitch. With Ultra-Blue® Lady Clairol it's a breeze. So quick and easy. Ultra-Blue Lady Clairol is that gentle, creamy hair lightener that feels deliciously cool going on, leaves hair in wonderful condition, softer-toned, dreamy. So if your hair is dull blonde or mousey brown and your life seems mousey brown, why hesitate? You could be enjoying every beautiful blonde advantage right now! Try Ultra-Blue Lady Clairol Creme Hair Lightener. The original Whipped Creme and Instant Whip® Lady Clairol are also available.

Your hairdresser will tell you a blonde's best friend is **Lady Clairol**® Creme Hair Lightener ©Clairol Inc., 1964

Plate 80

If I've only life

Plate 81

me live it as a blonde!™

...en, I was always a blonde at heart!
...very woman?
...ast I look like I like—and I love it!
...a joy. Remember Helen of Troy? She
...e blonde who launched a thousand
...(Cleopatra only had a barge.) So
...now to bewitch now!
...n Ultra-Blue Lady Clairol, it's so easy.
...Blue is that quick, cool, gentle hair
...er that really cares for your hair.

Achieves the soft-toned, dreamier blonde look
destined to turn heads, launch ships or just
change dull, mousey hair into irresistible
blonde appeal.

So if you're a blonde at heart, be a blonde
in fact. Act! Get Ultra-Blue Lady Clairol
and try it alone . . . or with Clairol™ Creme
Toner*. The glamour you'll feel is for real!
Your hairdresser will tell you a blonde's best
friend is Lady Clairol.

Ultra-Blue® Lady Clairol®

The closer he gets...the better you look!*

Now! Shampoo-in Hair Color so natural it invites close-ups!*

Let distance lend enchantment—to other women! You be the gal who looks even lovelier close up! Fresher, prettier, more exciting when your hair glows with the soft, natural-looking color of new Nice'n Easy by Clairol. Here is an easy-to-do, once-a-month shampoo-in

haircoloring so rich in formula, it can lighten lighter, brighten brighter...and deepen more evenly! So ri it covers gray better than any other shampoo-in co ...so rich, it leaves your hair with lively body...and exciting glow! Try it for a lift...for the confiden deep inside, of knowing your beautiful hair color lo "so natural it invites close-ups"!

The closer he gets...the better you loo

Plate 82

Pour it on...
work it through.

Wait just minutes...
rinse...shampoo!

Nice 'n Easy...
so natural looking!

New!
Nice 'n Easy®
by Clairol

**the natural-looking hair color
you just shampoo in!**

*Trademark   © Clairol Inc. 1966

women, 'Does she or doesn't she use hair coloring?'" Agency men being notoriously persuadable, all hands agreed that Miss Polykoff was cleanminded and sincere. And after all, they had hired her because she could write for women.

At Clairol, Inc., which is now a division of Bristol-Myers but was then independent and run by a triumvirate of the founding father and his two sons, one of the sons loved the line, while his brother and father were willing to go along with it. (The son who loved it is now president of Bristol-Myers, and his brother is executive vice-president.)

The first ads were scheduled to run in *Life* magazine, which then had to face its own little real-life drama: "Will we . . . or won't we run it?" It was too suggestive, they felt, and the answer was, they wouldn't. Miss Polykoff, whose Jewish motherism comes through from time to time ("How did I persuade them? You ought to know me, that's how."), realized suddenly that "We had it made; we could count on all men reading the ads for sheer shock value, like *Lolita* or *Fanny Hill.* And we had another, even greater advantage, with women. We knew that most of the women we wanted to influence had been brought up, as we had been, to believe it wasn't nice to admit, out loud anyway, that a nice girl ever got an off-color meaning about anything, especially in mixed company. So you see, almost everything can be turned into an advantage."

Life had researched the ad's dirtiness quotient among its all-male experts, who had turned it down, so Miss Polykoff challenged them to do their research among their women employees instead. Sure enough, they couldn't find one woman who would admit to getting a double meaning from the words, and, consciences salved, *Life* agreed to run it *(Plate 79).*

From the first, Miss Polykoff's advertising insisted that it is not unnatural to color your hair, that it is fun, and that it is eminently respectable. Almost every Miss Clairol ad has shown the woman model with a child snuggled up to her. This emphasis on Clairol users being happily married mothers (one ad reads: "Are mothers getting younger . . . or do they just look that way?"), combined with beautiful photographs and a teasing headline, is enough to make almost any woman accept the idea of using the product. In fact, when Miss Polykoff first wrote the "Does she . . . or doesn't she" line, it was originally answered with "So natural, only her Mother knows for sure." Miss Polykoff thought "Mother" was cuter than "hairdresser," but changed it so as not to offend the beauty salon market.

The one thing she did *not* do, however, was oversimplify the product. Miss Clairol and its competitors are dyes which change the color of the hair until it grows out again, and it is not easy to undo a hair coloring job. She recognized that hair coloring does change a woman's looks—

often drastically—in the same way that a nose job does, though at about one one-hundredth the price, and she made the results worth the trouble. "What's the point of buying the stuff," she says, "if it isn't going to change your life? Why would you go through all that, put all that crap on your head, unless you feel you're going to come out looking gorgeous?"

Over the past ten years, Clairol has added a number of hair-coloring products to its line, and Miss Polykoff has written similar catch-headlines for most of them *(Plates 80–82)*.

The campaign has of course been a great success: by 1967 more than 40 per cent of all American women had at least tried hair colorings, and, as is shown below, most of them had tried Clairol.

1955:	Hair coloring market sales	$ 25 million
	Clairol sales	3 million
	FCB Clairol billing	400 thousand
1969:	Hair coloring market sales	136 million
	Clairol sales	84 million
	FCB Clairol billing	35 million

¡ Que viva Sigmund Freud!

6

New Directions in Advertising

The New Humor

IT WAS WILLIAM BERNBACH who first looked at his client's product the way
a consumer would, in the context of a world that did not crumble if,
God forbid, there was no more Lifebuoy in the bathroom. When the
product had shortcomings (e.g. Avis, Volkswagen, Levy's), he recognized
them and used them to explain what its strengths were. The early
Volkswagen ads, like "Lemon," "Think small," "Is Volkswagen contemplating
a change?" were deliberate puns on the image of the car.

Bernbach was essentially whimsical, however, and the first real humorist
of the new advertising was Stan Freberg, a Los Angeles-based comedy
writer and actor who began doing very free campaigns in the mid-1950s.
One of his first clients was Butter-Nut Coffee, which in 1958 was about
to introduce its own brand of instant coffee, some five years after most
of its competitors had gone on the market with theirs. The problem, of
course, was trying to make people care, even a little bit, about still
another brand. Freberg did it this way:

On Thursday, July 1, 1958, a commercial ran on every Los Angeles
television station featuring an interview at L.A. International Airport
with Homer K. Butternut, president of the Butter-Nut Coffee Company.
Mr. Butternut had apparently arrived from Omaha with his family to
watch history's first attempt at nighttime skywriting.

It seems that Mr. Butternut had engaged Winfield (Ace) Jenkins, the
famous pilot, to make the skywriting attempt, which would be sponsored
by Butter-Nut. Jenkins was preparing to write across the night sky the
immortal words: "New Instant Butter-Nut Coffee is the first instant
coffee that tastes like coffee ought to taste."

The attempt was to be made at 10:30 P.M. the next Monday, and all
weekend there were interviews with Jenkins and Butternut, on both
radio and television, giving progress reports on the preparations. It
was announced that Jenkins would write the message on channels 2, 5, 7,
and 11 at precisely 10:30 P.M.

On Monday night, at the appointed time, Mr. Butternut appeared on all
four television channels, waiting with the rest of Los Angeles for Jenkins
to do his stuff. The tension built as reporters and cameramen crowded
around, all necks craned to the sky.

"Here he comes!" said Butternut, and there was a long, long *swooosshh*
as Jenkins's plane came by just off-camera, followed by a thick cloud of
smoke that completely obscured everybody. Butternut finally beat his
way out of the smoke to cry, "Too low, Jenkins, too low!"

Although Jenkins tried his best every night that week, he never made
it, perhaps because, as one of the Butter-Nut print ads said, "Skywriting

on television is a feat which might best be compared to canoeing on radio."

Freberg has made a career of special-purpose campaigns, mostly of short duration. In 1961 he introduced printed fortunes on the tags of Salada tea bags, then staged a gypsy tea-leaf readers' strike against the company for unfair competition. Gypsy wagons were parked outside the Salada plant in Newton, Mass., campfires burning through the night, and both sides ran ads in *The New Yorker* explaining their positions: "Who threw the gypsies out of work?" was the first, paid for by the gypsies. It was followed by "Salada's position in the gypsy strike." The third and final ad was the announcement: "Gypsy strike settled," which called for the gypsies to have control over the content of the tags.

Freberg's creations were among the first pieces of advertising humor that did not depend on making fun of a client's product—the approach of comedians like Fred Allen and Jack Benny—but instead were based on the observation that Americans respond to the illusions which they see on the face of a television set, or hear on the radio, or feel on the shelves of a supermarket, with as great a suspension of disbelief as that experienced by the reader of a novel. Recalling Orson Welles' famous broadcast of H. G. Wells' *The War of the Worlds* in 1938, when the entire country was panicked by the reported landing of Martians in southern New Jersey, Freberg has proved his point by using radio for jobs that most people would consider impossible: he once drained Lake Erie of all its water, then filled it with an immense scoop of chocolate ice cream, poured marshmallow sauce over it from Buffalo to Detroit, topped it with whipped cream, and then added a maraschino cherry the size of Toledo.

Freberg does not run an agency, and will not handle general advertising for his clients; and most agencies, for their part, could not sustain the kind of humor that Freberg depends on. One, however, has used humor with marked success, and that is Wells, Rich, Greene.

Wells, Rich, Greene's style is close to that of Carl Ally, and some of its work seems derivative of Ally's campaigns for Volvo and Hertz. The most famous of the agency's first campaigns was for Philip Morris's Benson & Hedges 100-millimeter cigarettes. "From the beginning," says Mary Wells Lawrence, the agency's president, "we have stressed only one point: our cigarettes are longer than king size. We show it over and over again."

In the first commercial, a disembodied voice announces: "The disadvantages of smoking Benson & Hedges 100s." On the screen, two men are in earnest conversation at a cocktail party. One of them has a long, carefully-trimmed goatee; the other, short and intense, is smoking a Benson & Hedges 100. As he speaks, we see that his cigarette is so long that it is burning the beard of his friend, who now seems to smell the acrid fumes and feel the heat. Just as they both realize what the matter is, the film cuts to: a Benson & Hedges smoker being squeezed into a crowded elevator. He cannot get his hand up in time to remove the cigarette and prevent the doors from closing on it. Cut to: a potter at his wheel, Benson & Hedges dangling from his lips as he shapes a vase. He turns to one side for a moment, then looks back to discover that he has implanted his cigarette in the side of his vase. Cut to: a rock climber, hanging by his rope over an awesome chasm, Benson & Hedges in his mouth. As he looks for a foothold, we see that his cigarette is burning a hole through his rope. He turns around just as the rope burns through, and drops from sight. End of commercial.

These tableaux-vivants come right out of the great days of silent movies. The product is neither glorified nor denigrated, but rather used simply as the mechanical element on which the joke turns, much as Keaton, in *The General,* used the railway cannon mounted on a flatcar, which drooped at the wrong moments and aimed itself at him instead of the Union soldiers; and as Chaplin, in *The Cure,* used a gin-filled health-spa fountain for his teetotaling ladies to drink from. Advertising, the great borrower, seems finally to have learned from whom to borrow.

Advertising and Political Action

All major political candidates today use advertising to help get their names, faces, positions and, hopefully, charisma across to the voters. Some of the advertising is reasonably honest, refraining from hyperbole and overt lies. Some of it is misdirected, appearing over the candidate's signature but obviously written in a style far different from his own. (A glaring example was New York Governor Nelson Rockefeller's 1968 campaign for the Republican presidential nomination. The ads were written by Jack Tinker & Partners, sounded nothing like Rockefeller, and cost more than $5 million.) Much of it, however, is immoral and cannot be justified by any democratic standard.

William Bernbach, who made his reputation by stressing honest appraisals of his clients' products, was perhaps the worst offender. In the 1964 presidential campaign, his television commercials for President Johnson included one ten-second spot that showed a little girl counting daisy petals. As she pulls them off, a voice is counting down to zero, at which point she is obliterated by an atomic-bomb explosion. The message, delivered without evidence to support its thesis, was that anyone who voted for Barry Goldwater would be unleashing the man who would destroy the world. "We took the Johnson account," Bernbach said later, "because we felt that if Mr. Goldwater won, it would have been dangerous for this country. Having that feeling, it was fair to run the commercial."

This attitude gives some indication of how little, after all, even the leaders of the new advertising have changed from the days when the only morality was the success of one's client's product.

The campaigns in this section are political only in the larger sense that advocacy of a position on a moral or social issue is a political action. In the case of the New York Civilian Complaint Review Board, the campaign against the Board made a political issue of the administrative structure of the city's Police Department, giving voters an opportunity to express themselves on the rights of citizens and policemen. To many people, the campaign forced the issue between bigots and racists, on one side, and so-called liberals on the other. It required every voter to make a conscious decision, in the voting booth, as to which side he was on. It is not often that the American voter gets to make that choice.

The second campaign, for the Sierra Club, is one of those freak acts of genius that occasionally come along to save the advertising business from its own polluted nature, and help restore a bit of dignity to those who don't even realize they have none. Very few in the business would have had the courage to attempt it, much less the talent to succeed.

The campaign really is a monument to the man who, though he did not write it, made it possible: the late Howard Luck Gossage. Gossage, who died of leukemia in 1969, was for years the only real humanist in advertising. He was a marvelously talented essayist, with a spacious style that resembled Robert Benchley's enriched with a bit of S. J. Perelman. A gadfly on moral issues related to the advertising industry (the right of minorities to full news coverage, the fact that news media are subsidized by their advertisers rather than by their readers), Gossage was the man who brought Marshall McLuhan to the United States and recognized the importance of what he had to say—though Gossage might have said it better. And, finally, he was the man who hired Jerry Mander, a young San Francisco public relations writer, who has since become what one admirer describes as "Bill Bernbach with balls."

The final campaign in the book was created by the American Cancer Society, and it marks the death of cigarette advertising in this country. Much of the story has less to do with advertising than with the infighting in Congress, and in the Federal Trade Commission and the Federal Communications Commission, over the issue of banning cigarette advertising and/or sales in this country; and with the enormous campaign of lobbying and arm-twisting by the cigarette manufacturers trying to preserve their business. That story, unfortunately, is just beginning to come out, and much information is still unavailable. It should make interesting reading.

The Police vs. the People

In New York City, where more Irish still swear allegiance to Sinn Fein than in all of Ireland, and where more Italians cover up for the Mafia than in all of Sicily, the age of the Holy War is not yet over. In the fall of 1966 these two groups, who even in Rome are looked upon as right-wing deviationists, allied themselves briefly with their traditional enemy, the Jewish Storekeeper, and took on the Forces of Evil in a bloody battle to the finish: the campaign to abolish the Civilian Complaint Review Board. The Forces of Evil, naturally, were the Colored, the Spanish and the Rich Jews, all led by the Anti-Christ Himself, Mayor John Lindsay.

The Civilian Complaint Review Board was Lindsay's attempt at building black and Puerto Rican confidence in the New York Police Department, which has traditionally drawn most of its men, and its attitudes, from the Irish and Italian communities. Although reasonably honest, and reasonably efficient without undue brutality in its work, the department—like most other white organizations—has been unable to respond quickly enough to the new challenges posed by ghetto blacks who now are beginning to exercise political and physical power in the city. Although Police Department heads have for years gone out of their way to recruit Negroes for the department, and have conducted seminars in community relations and the sociology and pathology of ghetto life for all new patrolmen—even including the sending of dozens of men at a time to Puerto Rico to observe an alien culture—the approach has tended to be based on the premise that Respect for Law and Order is as important a virtue as Respect for One's Parents; it is an article of faith as strong as that of the Virgin Birth. The premise falls apart, however, when applied to ghetto children of poverty-stricken, semiliterate, unstable households, who are forced as adolescents and adults to confront the blank wall of white middle-class values.

When the board was proposed by Lindsay during his election campaign in 1965, it was enthusiastically supported by the city's intellectuals, including Lindsay's political coalition of Reform Democrats, Yale Republicans, and the white liberal establishment, who joined together with Negro civil rights leaders ranging from the Maoists on the left to Whitney Young on the right. Leading the opposition was the Patrolmen's Benevolent Association, an informal union of most of the city's policemen, and the Conservative party, a right-wing offshoot of the Republicans. They spoke for most of the city's Catholics, nominally Democrats but notoriously bigoted on social issues, and they were joined in the fight by the Jewish taxi drivers and candy-store owners. The city's 750,000 Puerto Ricans, though not organized or vocal, were assumed to be in favor of the board, particularly as the few prominent Puerto Ricans in city affairs were on Lindsay's side.

The Civilian Complaint Review Board, as Lindsay set it up, investigated complaints made against the city's policemen for brutality, incorrect or illegal actions, and the like; the board could, if it found them justified, recommend to the Police Commissioner that he take disciplinary action against the offending policemen. Such a recommendation would be noted on the policeman's career record and could have an adverse effect on future promotions. If the board found that the complaint was not justified, it would notify the Commissioner of this, and the entire incident, including the original complaint, would be removed from the policeman's record on the ground that it might unfairly affect his career. All investigations would be conducted by policemen attached to the Review Board.

This board differed in only three respects from one that had been in operation for years within the Police Department. First, it expanded the board from five members to seven. Second, it proposed that four of the seven be "civilians"—that is, not members of the Police Department. Third, it added the protection that a policeman unjustly accused by a complainant would not have the record of that complaint attached to him for the rest of his career. The board would have no power to punish, nor could it even recommend a specific punishment to the Commissioner.

In retrospect, the Civilian Complaint Review Board was hardly the revolutionary instrument both sides made it out to be. It had no powers that were not already vested in the existing board, it could not punish policemen, and, in fact, gave them some protections that the existing board did not.

Nevertheless, when Lindsay took office in January of 1966 and a few months later appointed the board, his opponents began a campaign for its removal that was unparalleled in the city's history for its brutality, its appeal to racism, and its absolutely blind hatred of those known to be or suspected of being in favor of it. John Cassese, the head of the Patrolmen's Benevolent Association, said: "Communism and Communists are somewhere mixed up in this fight. If the Communists are not in the forefront, they are somewhere in the middle, making hay while the sun shines."

The opposition's first step was to put the question of the board's continued existence in the form of a referendum to be voted on in the November, 1966 elections. (The referendum was worded so that a "yes" vote would abolish the board, a "no" vote would keep it. It was said by supporters of the board that this was dirty pool, that ignorant voters who

Plate 83

This is the aftermath of a riot in a city that <u>had</u> a civilian review board

Following these riots, the Federal Bureau of Investigation reported to the President of the United States:

"**Where there is an outside Civilian Review Board, the restraint of the police was so great that effective action against the rioters appeared to be impossible. In short, the police were so careful to avoid accusations of improper conduct that they were virtually paralyzed.**"

John J. Harrington, ex-policeman, president of the Fraternal Order of Police, testified before the Court of Common Pleas in Philadelphia on the effect of the Police Advisory Board during the riots of 1964. (Philadelphia's Police Advisory Board is the equivalent of Mayor Lindsay's Civilian Review Board.) He repeated much of this before the Marchi State Senate committee hearings in New York City. His Philadelphia testimony, in part, is as follows:

"*The riot ran wild day and night for four days... I think the city itself recognized the effect of the Police Advisory Board on the Police Department during that riot... I got a* phone call from the City Manager, and he told me that the Mayor was going to read the proclamation... the riot act... and when the Mayor did, that the policemen would have the authority... to use whatever force they deemed necessary to enforce that police order.... I questioned if they would be taken before the Advisory Board for their actions... Mr. Fred Corleto, present City Manager... put the City Solicitor on the phone, Mr. Bauer... Mr. Bauer assured me that the policemen, once the riot act was read... could issue a police order and use sufficient force to enforce that order... their actions wouldn't be taken before the Police Advisory Board... after I gave this message to the policemen, **in four hours the riot was over**...

We had the worst riot in 1964 right here in the City of Philadelphia, and the City of Rochester had the second worst riot, **and they were the only two cities at that time that had Police Advisory Boards; so they are not safety valves.**"

Crime and violence are the terrifying realities of our time. No street is safe. No neighbor- hood is immune. New York's police force, probably the finest in the world, is all that stands ready to protect you and your family from the ominous threat of constant danger in the streets. A police officer must not feel that his every action is being judged by non-professionals on the Lindsay Civilian Review Board. He must not feel that his job, pension or reputation can be jeopardized. He must feel free to take swift and direct action when danger strikes. New York is waging a total war against crime. To win it, we must depend on a totally effective police department capable of providing total protection to every citizen.

Mayor Lindsay's Civilian Review Board hampers a police officer in the performance of his duty. It is a weight that must be lifted. He must not feel doubt. He must not pause... even for an instant. It could mean your life. Vote to stop the Civilian Review Board. Tuesday, November 8th—vote "YES!" on Question #1.

INDEPENDENT CITIZENS COMMITTEE AGAINST CIVILIAN REVIEW BOARDS

Stop the Civilian Review Board! November 8th—Vote "<u>YES!</u>" on Question #1.

Plate 84

wanted to keep the board might vote "yes" by mistake; but no attempt was ever made by the opposition to deceive anyone. The alternatives were always spelled out clearly.)

Cassese was an amiable patrolman who had made his career in the politics of the Police Department. He and the PBA's public-relations man, Norman Frank, were both immensely talented at getting what they conceived to be the greatest gains for their policemen. They levied a tax of $5 on every member of the PBA, with contributions also encouraged at American Legion halls, Knights of Columbus meetings, and church bingo evenings, to pay for the referendum's legal and advertising costs. Altogether, about $600,000 was raised—a large sum, though not nearly as much as their opponents accused them of spending.

Supporters of the board—though the most articulate people in New York—were unable to agree on how to handle their side of the campaign, could not raise money for it, and ended up with no plan at all.

In early September, Norman Frank hired Cole, Fischer, Rogow, a small advertising agency. Larry Marks, vice-president and creative director of the agency, was put in charge of the advertising. Marks was probably the last man in New York one would think of to lead the PBA's campaign. An upper-middle-class New York Jew in his early forties, he played tennis at lunchtime and counted among his friends a number of articulate theater and show-business people.

He said later that when he first heard about the proposed PBA campaign he had no strong feelings one way or the other about the board and didn't know how he might have voted. But he took on the job of researching the problem for the PBA, "just like any other client. The more research I did, the more involved I became, the more convinced I was that crime in the streets was the reality that we had to deal with."

"Crime in the streets" has been a euphemism in America for years, standing for "black crime in the streets." White crime in the streets is referred to by its proper name: assault, robbery or mugging, for example. Marks, however, chose to build his campaign on that phrase, and by doing so he was able to organize the votes of everyone who knew what the phrase really stood for. "Good advertising," he said, "must be based on apprehension. . . . People wanted freedom from fear in the streets. Our basic concern was with the morale of the Police Department. It seemed to us that the police needed a show of confidence from the public. Would you take a job on the police force? I wouldn't—get a bullet in the back of the head walking down the street! So our story, that the people of the city were threatened by crime, and that the Police Department had to be supported, was more important than the question of anything a civilian review board could do for ethnic minority groups."

The first ad ran in late September, and was an excellent distillation

Why did the minister resign from Philadelphia's civilian review board?

The following testimony by Reverend W. Carter Merbrier is directly from the court records in Philadelphia where hearings are now in progress to determine the value of the civilian review board in that city.

"Most cases involved criminal elements bringing in policemen in an attempt to have their records expunged...a lot of people came before the board almost with a sense of revenge...the NAACP was going to bypass it... I believe sincerely in my heart that the review board was accomplishing nothing...I believe it should be dissolved."

Reverend Merbrier, a most compassionate and civic minded citizen of Philadelphia, was not passing hasty judgment. He served diligently on the board for two and a half years.

Another Philadelphian, businessman Mr. Joseph Glennon, resigned after eighteen months on the board. He felt that it wasted the time of police officers. Mr. Glennon further testified:

"It is just an opportunity for questionable characters to vent grudges against the police."

Safety in the streets is the real issue of this campaign against the Lindsay Civilian Review Board. Crime is rising seven times faster than the increase in population. Last year, in our city, there were over **1500 rapes**, more than **16,000 felonious assaults**, almost **9,000 robberies**, over **600 murders**, and, incredible as it may read, over **160,000 felonies**. Yes, our great city is plagued by crime, and the battle against it must be waged by a totally effective police force.

Philadelphia policemen testify that they do hesitate

Can a civilian review board hamper a policeman in the performance of his duty? The Philadelphia court records include the following testimony from members of the police force.

Policeman Virgil Penn, Jr.: *"When [the board] builds up this reluctance in a man's mind and makes him hesitate to do his duty, something real serious may happen...he has no time to pull a book out of his pocket to see if he is doing it properly...I think it [the board] creates a mental block in the policeman's mind...he builds up this reluctance in his mind that if he does [his duty] he is going to suffer recriminations...he would lose pay...he would lose part of his livelihood, and it would affect his family at home. This I think destroys the morale of the policemen."*

Policeman Howard Hall: *"...with the pressure that has been applied to me I would say that... the less I do, the less trouble I'm going to get into, and I act accordingly...I do as little as possible, within reason...I can only take the path of least resistance when I'm out on the street...the Advisory Board was completely demoralizing."*

Detective Edward Saltzman: *"It's very demoralizing. It can really get to you after a while... they [the police] don't know which way to turn."*

Policeman Constant Helvitson: *"If we can't do our job, it's not worth it."*

Policeman Alfred Sulvetta: *"It just makes you feel like 'Can I go out and do this job? Or should I rack up (resign) now?'"*

Policeman William Harvey: *"It is a deterrent to doing your job...you have this in the back of your mind at all times..."*

The policeman is all that stands between you, your family and the constant threat of violence. He must not feel that his integrity is being judged every time he acts. A policeman must not fear that his job, pension or reputation can be threatened by a board of non-professionals.

If Mayor Lindsay's Civilian Review Board deters one officer from the performance of his duty...it could mean your life. He must not feel doubt. He must not pause...even for an instant. Vote to stop the Civilian Review Board. Tuesday, November 8th—vote "YES!" on Question #1.

INDEPENDENT CITIZENS COMMITTEE AGAINST CIVILIAN REVIEW BOARDS

Stop the Civilian Review Board! November 8th—Vote "YES!" on Question #1.

Plate 85

of this point of view *(Plate 83)*. The reaction it got was astounding. No one in the history of New York politics had ever before called a spade a nigger, and here it was in *The New York Times,* yet. Dick Schaap, a columnist for another New York paper, the *World Journal Tribune,* wrote:

. . . The implication, quite clearly, is that if you don't send in your contribution today [to the Independent Citizens' Committee], the Civilian Review Board, individually and collectively, is going to rape the poor girl.

. . . The problem with the ad, I'm afraid, is that only intellectuals are going to grasp its sly nuances. In the future, the Independent Citizen's Committee will just have to be more explicit. Take the same setting. Have the white girl emerging from the subway and show 14 Negroes, wearing fezes, hypodermic needles hanging from their arms, descending upon her with sub-machine guns. In the background, show four well-scrubbed policemen thinking. They are thinking about whether or not they should arrest the 14 aspiring assassins and risk the wrath of the Civilian Review Board, which would not understand such action. For emphasis, in case the message doesn't get across, members of the Civilian Review Board could be shown holding back the officers.

This is the real message of the Independent Citizens' Committee Against Civilian Review Boards, and they should be willing to spell it out.

Theodore Kheel, a well known labor mediator in New York and a civilian member of the board, commented:

The ad does not specifically say, but the message is clear: if attacked, this girl can expect little help from the police because of their fear of not getting a fair hearing if a complaint of misconduct is filed. This implication is demonstrably false. . . . It is, moreover, an unwarranted slur on the police to suggest that they would fail to come to the help of this girl, or anyone, under any circumstances.

By the time of the election the issue before the voters was clear to all: a vote to retain the Civilian Complaint Review Board was an expression of support for blacks who wanted to have a recognized, official forum in which to express their grievances. A vote against the board was a denial of that demand. John Cassese said: "We are sick and tired of giving in to minority groups with their gripes and shouting."

The Cole, Fischer, Rogow campaign continued through October with newspaper ads and radio and television commercials *(Plates 84–88)*.

The board's supporters, though infuriated by the PBA ads (Kheel said: "First of all, the name of the board is not the Civilian Review Board as the ad states. It is the Civilian *Complaint* Review Board. . . . It is not a civilian board to review police actions, but a police board to review civilian complaints"), were never able to work effectively. They put together an acronymous group called FAIR—Federated Association for Impartial Review—which turned out some rather amateurish ads aimed at people who already were on their side. FAIR was hampered also by having to rely on a budget erratically donated by a few affluent liberals. The ads were hastily prepared, and were run whenever enough new donations came in.

It is doubtful, however, whether *any* ads or *any* budget would have helped very much. Mayor Lindsay was out stumping the city every day in the face of advice from his aides to the effect that "We can't win the fight. Why lose it?" Lindsay replied to one newsman, "I've done a lot of things that I've wondered about whether they were the right things; but I have no doubts about this one." Governor Rockefeller, Senators Jacob Javits and Robert Kennedy, and even the Police Commissioner all made strong statements supporting the board, and all received wide publicity. Every newspaper in New York except the *Daily News,* and many radio and television stations, took editorial positions supporting Lindsay and the board, and news coverage of the issue rivaled that of the concurrent statewide campaign for governor. A few days before the election, with all signs pointing toward a defeat for the board, columnist Jimmy Breslin wrote a piece in the *World Journal Tribune:*

They are my people, the police of the City of New York. I have been raised with them. I know them and I love them. On Tuesday they apparently are going to win a referendum which will abolish the Civilian Review Board. And now my people have to become my enemies because nobody who carries a gun can be allowed to have the power, even the hint of the power, that this referendum on Tuesday will give them.

. . . In November, 1966, the month the white backlash becomes a fact, you can say anything, as long as the words promise to contain Negroes.

Up until the day before the election, the advertising done by the board's supporters received little attention. But on that Monday, an ad appeared in *The New York Times* written by Richard Gilbert of Gilbert Advertising Agency and Martin Smith of Smith/Greenland, and signed by thirty prominent advertising people in New York, attacking Cole, Fischer, Rogow's campaign for the PBA. The ad accused the agency of perverting the purposes of advertising, and of writing deliberately false and misleading ads *(Plate 89).*

The next day the Civilian Complaint Review Board was defeated by a vote of 3 to 2. The boroughs of Queens and Staten Island, heavily white and Catholic, voted more than 3 to 1 against the board. Although Negroes voted better than 6 to 1 in favor of it, the Jews, traditionally the city's liberals, divided much more closely than expected, with professionals going one way and storekeepers the other. The Puerto Ricans, whom everyone had expected to vote with the Negroes, were almost evenly divided — a great shock to those liberals who had forgotten the conservative, Catholic traditions of this group.

All mothers wait up at night!

We can't take chances... not with our children!

New York City is plagued by crime. The streets are no longer safe. Those who oppose our position claim we are sponsoring a campaign of fear. If they will refute the facts presented, we will discontinue our campaign. But they can't, because facts are facts.

The crime rate is rising seven times faster than the increase in population. Last year in our city, statistics reveal this staggering list of crimes:

MURDERS	634
RAPES	1,574
ROBBERIES	8,904
FELONIOUS ASSAULTS	16,325
TOTAL FELONIES	166,075

We cannot afford to provide our families with less than total police protection!

The issue to be dealt with is "safety in the streets." The question is whether or not a police force operating under a civilian review board can perform with total effectiveness.

The Federal Bureau of Investigation says IT CANNOT.

A minister, a college professor, a businessman who have just resigned from Philadelphia's civilian complaint review board say IT CANNOT.

John J. Harrington, president of Philadelphia's Fraternal Order of Police says IT CANNOT.

Is it possible that policemen, intimidated by a civilian review board, will use undue caution in the performance of their duty? Honor policemen testifying under oath before the Court of Common Pleas in Philadelphia swore that they **have** hesitated.

The policeman is all that stands between you, your family and the mounting threat of violence. He must not feel doubt. He must not pause . . . even for an instant. Vote to abolish Mayor Lindsay's Civilian Review Board. Tuesday, November 8th—vote "YES!" on Question #1.

**INDEPENDENT CITIZENS COMMITTEE
AGAINST CIVILIAN REVIEW BOARDS**

Stop the Civilian Review Board! November 8th—Vote "YES!" on Question #1.

Plate 86

Plate 87

(THE COMMERCIAL STARTS WITH SOUNDS OF CRASHING GLASS, AND THEN SOUNDS OF A RIOT, WHICH CONTINUE THROUGH THE FIRST LINE OF THE ANNOUNCER'S SPEECH.)

ANNOUNCER: You are listening to the sound track of a riot, a riot that went completely out of control. At the time, the police of that city were subject to the jurisdiction of a Civilian Review Board. Following these riots, the Federal Bureau of Investigation reported to the President of the United States:

SECOND MALE VOICE: Where there is an outside Civilian Review Board, the restraint of the police was so great that effective action against the rioters appeared to be impossible. In short, the police were so careful to avoid accusations of improper conduct that they were virtually paralyzed.

FIRST ANNOUNCER: Crime and violence are the terrifying realities of our time. The police must not be hampered in the performance of their duty. Vote 'yes' to abolish the Civilian Review Board. Vote 'yes' to stop the politically appointed, nonprofessional Civilian Review Board. The police need your total support. You need their total protection. Stop the Civilian Review Board. Vote 'yes' on Question number one.

At the victory celebration, Norman Frank announced gratuitously to the city that he could personally promise all citizens that the police would not abuse their new power, which was of course what the whole fight had been about. And at first the police did not abuse their power; the election seemed to have been a purgative for the city. The act of pulling the lever down in the voting booth was release enough for the emotions generated by the campaign.

Lindsay and Police Commissioner Leary tried to salvage something from the defeat; a month after the election Leary enlarged his complaint review board (the one that had always been in existence) from five members to seven, and appointed four of its members from among the civilian employees of the Police Department, including two high-ranking consultants in community relations. Not a word of opposition was heard, even from the PBA, perhaps because it knew what would happen with an all-police board: in the two years following the election, through the summer of 1968, the board investigated more than 2,200 civilian complaints against policemen and dismissed all but seven.

Cole, Fischer, Rogow brought an $8 million libel and slander suit

1. ANNCR: (VO) The addict,

2. the criminal,

3. the hooligan.

4. These are the enemies that threaten your safety.

5. Crime is faceless.

6. Crime is a virus infecting our city.

7. No neighborhood is immune.

8. Every street has become a playground of terror.

9. The crime rate is rising

10. seven times faster than the increase in population.

11. Only the policeman stand between you

12. and this threat of mounting violence.

13. Your life can depend on his swift and decisive action.

14. He must not feel doubt.

15. He must not pause even for an instant.

16. If he fears that positive action may be misinterpreted

17. by non-professionals on the Civilian Review Board

18. it could mean your life.

19. Vote to stop the Civilian Review Board. Vote yes on question number one.

Plate 88

Plate 89

174

This message is neither for nor against the Civilian Review Board. It is against a certain type of advertising.

When integrity, taste and discretion are the losers — who wins? Appeals to passion, and the use of deceptive inflammatory statements in the advertising campaign by the Independent Citizens Committee Against Civilian Review Boards only confuse and frighten the public and make reasoned judgment difficult.

When advertising is used solely to exploit and incite emotion, our craft is dishonored and damage is done to advertising prudence and credibility.

This advertisement is sponsored by the following members of the advertising industry:

Carl Ally, Carl Ally, Inc.
Altman, Stoller, Chalk
Stephen Baker, Mogul Baker Byrne Weiss Inc.
Paul Becker, Auerbach & Becker, Inc.
Robert T. Colwell, J. Walter Thompson Co.
Maxwell Dane
John de Garmo, de Garmo Inc.
Elliot Unger & Elliot
Richard L. Gilbert, Gilbert Advertising Agency, Inc.
H. Victor Grohmann, Needham & Grohmann, Inc.
Helitzer, Waring & Wayne, Inc.
Daniel S. Karsch, Daniel & Charles, Inc.
Shepard Kurnit, Delehanty, Kurnit & Geller Inc.
Robert Larimer, Nadler & Larimer, Inc.
Richard K. Manoff, Richard K. Manoff, Inc.

J. M. Mathes Inc.
David B. McCall, LaRoche, McCaffrey and McCall, Inc.
Pace Advertising Agency, Inc.
Pampel & Associates, Inc.
Shirley Polykoff, Foote, Cone & Belding, Inc.
Irwin Ress, Norrito, Ress Inc.
Murray H. Salit, Salit & Garlanda, Inc.
The Shaller Rubin Co., Inc.
Smith/Greenland Co., Inc.
Martin Solow, Solow/Wexton, Inc.
Leonard Spring, Ted Gravenson, Inc.
Jane Trahey, Trahey Advertising, Inc.
Albert D. Van Brunt, Van Brunt & Co.
Walter Weir, West, Weir & Bartel, Inc.
Lester Wunderman, Wunderman, Ricotta & Kline, Inc.

against the thirty individuals and agencies who had signed the election eve ad, and a $1 million suit against Smith and Gilbert, claiming that they had damaged Cole, Fischer, Rogow's professional standing. In the spring of 1968 the suits were dismissed by the courts on the ground that the ad was fair comment on the campaign.

In 1967, summing up his campaign for a reporter, Larry Marks made perhaps the most revealing statement of all: "You can't say," he said, "that everybody who voted our way was a bigot, because then you'd have a real problem on your hands." It would be hard to imagine a more accurate count.

The Sierra Club

Here is an interesting problem for the especially devoted advertising student to consider, but it requires a major suspension of disbelief on the student's part. Suppose, first of all, that in 1963 the federal government had built a dam across the Colorado River, just upstream from the Grand Canyon, without telling anyone about it (well, just suppose), and that the reservoir from that dam had flooded 150 miles of the wildest and most beautiful country in the continental United States, drowning it forever.

Then suppose that three years later, in 1966, the government proposed to build two more dams on the Colorado, farther downstream, whose waters would back up a hundred miles into the Grand Canyon, almost to the spot where tourists stand on the South Rim when they come to make their once-in-a-lifetime visit to this greatest of all natural wonders.

And, thirdly, suppose that Congress agreed with the government that this was a fine idea and was just about to pass the bill that would finance the new dams.

Finally, suppose that you had less than $50,000 to spend on an advertising campaign against the construction of the dams, and that you would have to make it so effective, and draw so much popular response, that the government would drop its proposed dams and Congress would refuse to appropriate the funds for constructing them.

What would you say in the ads?

What, indeed? That the problem is unreal and the solution impossible? That the idea of damming up the Grand Canyon—the *Grand Canyon*—is too—well—irrational? That everyone knows you can't just go around building dams in the Grand Canyon? After all, its . . . well, it's . . . it's the *Grand Canyon.* Sort of, you know, ours . . . the people's . . . and our children's . . . and, well . . . the world's. Right? Wrong. That is exactly what the government and Congress did, although you are not likely to have heard about it, since it all happened before the great ecology boom of 1970.

That was the advertising problem presented to Howard Gossage and Jerry Mander in May of 1966. It was brought to them by a man named David Brower, who was executive director of an organization of conservationists called the Sierra Club, which runs outings and camping trips to wilderness areas, and publishes beautiful books of photographs of these areas. It is also very concerned with saving what little remains of our unspoiled country.

Gossage and Mander, whose names are unknown even to many in the advertising business, operated out of a former firehouse in San Francisco. Until his death in 1969, Gossage presided over a loose confederation of talents who concerned themselves with advertising, product invention, publicity and anything else that sounded interesting. With Dr. Gerald Feigen, for example, who is a psychiatrist turned proctologist, Gossage publicized the 1967 bid for independence of the West Indian island of Anguilla, because he believed in the freedom of people to do and be as they wish, and believed that the world cannot refuse independence to anyone who wants it. He was a contributing editor of *Ramparts* magazine, and influenced much of its style and even its typography. Gossage invented Beethoven sweatshirts, and once wrote an Eagle Shirt ad for *The New Yorker* (asking for suggestions of new names for shirt colors) that drew 12,000 replies from a total circulation of 300,000. His own suggestions included Statutory Grape and Unforeseeable Fuchsia.

Mander first associated himself with Gossage in 1964, when at the age of twenty-eight he was doing publicity for the ill-fated Republican presidential campaign of Marvin Kitman. Kitman was running on the Republican platform of 1864, which he felt had not yet been implemented. That platform, it may be recalled, proposed freeing the slaves, bringing the South back into the Union, and reinforcing the garrison at Fort Sumter rather than elsewhere. Among Mander's other projects was his creation of the Great Paper Airplane Contest of 1966, a promotion for *Scientific American* magazine designed to attract airline advertisers. With two ads in *The New York Times*—in the first one he almost forgot to mention the name of the magazine—Mander got almost twelve thousand entries for the various divisions of his contest, including origami and distance flying (one entry was a hard round ball of papier-mâché, carrying the instruction that it was to be held in the hand and thrown as hard as possible in the direction of the finish line).

This is hardly the background one normally finds in a crusading conservationist, but Mander views the world from San Francisco, which is the only American city that has not yet obliterated its natural site with the usual lava flow of concrete embedded in asphalt. Its history of earthquakes seems to have made it uniquely responsive to vibrations of all kinds: hippies, topless dancers and Hell's Angels all have flourished there. For a city its size (Baltimore, Cleveland, Milwaukee and St. Louis all are larger), it has had a great influence on American life and mores, and is probably the only city whose gossip columnist (Herb Caen) is more influential than its mayor.

San Francisco is also the home of the Sierra Club, and Brower had been aware of Gossage's work for some time. "I remembered a piece Howard wrote in *Harper's,*" Brower recalled (actually an advertisement for Rover motorcars), "where he didn't like billboards or Smokey the Bear. This is the thing Howard and I have in common: we both hate Smokey. Smokey is the epitome of the evil that good men do. In man's attempt to keep his own property from burning, and to preserve nature as he sees it today, he forgets that forest fires are necessary to the natural order. Some species of plants (the fire-cone pine, for example) actually *need* forest fires to reproduce themselves. For thirty years we've kept forest fires out of the great Sequoia forests, thinking that they would kill the trees. But all that the fires used to do was clear out the dry, dead limbs that clogged up the forest floor. The trees weren't even touched. Now we have twenty feet of dry kindling in there, and if ever a fire comes—and it has to, sometime—the whole forest will be gone."

Gossage looked at it a different way. "Smokey looks surly, burly and pissed off. You know that if there's been a forest fire he thinks you set it."

In May of 1966 it seemed to Brower a foregone conclusion that the government would build its dams in the Grand Canyon. The dams were a pork-barrel project for Arizona, sponsored by Senator Carl Hayden (at eighty-nine, he was then the Senate's oldest living member, and had devoted much of his senatorial career to getting the dams built before he retired), and by Congressman Morris Udall, whose brother Stewart, ironically, was the conservationist Secretary of the Interior, charged with responsibility for protecting wilderness areas. Congressional logs were rolling all over the place and Udall and Hayden had the votes to put the dams through.

Brower felt that a public appeal, in the form of an advertisement, was the only weapon left against the dams. He asked Gossage and Mander if they would write an ad on behalf of the club. "The amount of money we could offer Howard was embarrassingly small: a $20,000 retainer for the first year, plus whatever we could scrape together for media charges."

The three men formed an odd triumvirate. Brower, who in his conservation battles could play Hector against the Achaeans, has devoted his entire adult life to the cause of the wilderness and, like Hector, has seen his territory shrink year by year under the assault of lumbermen, power companies, and mine owners. Gossage, the dilettante supreme, combined enormous verbal talent with the concentration span of a politician at an opponent's testimonial dinner. Mander, who looks like a Jewish fuzzy-wuzzy, has the talent of Gossage and the perseverance of Brower. Mander wrote the ads.

Mander is not an outdoorsman, has never been to the Grand Canyon, and would not be particularly upset if he never went. "But even if you *never* go to the Grand Canyon," he says, "or care to, if you're irrevocably committed to urban life, you're probably *still* outraged that anybody would even dream of doing anything to it."

So in May, 1966, Mander wrote the first ad, and selected the media in which it would appear. He had about $10,000 with which to buy

(If they can turn Grand Canyon into a "cash register"
is any national park safe? You know the answer.)

Now Only You Can Save Grand Canyon From Being Flooded...For Profit

Yes, that's right, *Grand Canyon!* The facts are these:

1. Bill H.R. 4671 is now before Rep. Wayne Aspinall's (Colo.) House Committee on Interior and Insular Affairs. This bill provides for two dams—Bridge Canyon and Marble Gorge—which would stop the Colorado River and flood water back into the canyon.

2. Should the bill pass, two standing lakes will fill what is presently 130 miles of canyon gorge. As for the wild, running Colorado River, the canyon's sculptor for 25,000,000 years, it will become dead water.

3. In some places the canyon will be submerged five hundred feet deep. "The most revealing single page of the earth's history," as Joseph Wood Krutch has described the fantastic canyon walls, will be drowned.

The new artificial shoreline will fluctuate on hydroelectric demand. Some days there will only be acres of mud where the flowing river and living canyon now are.

4. Why are these dams being built, then? For commercial power. They are dams of the sort which their sponsor, the Bureau of Reclamation of the Department of the Interior, calls "cash registers."

In other words, these dams aren't even to store water for people and farms, but to provide *auxiliary* power for industry. Arizona power politics in your Grand Canyon.

Moreover, Arizona doesn't need the dams to carry out its water development. Actually, it would have more water without the dams.

5. For, the most remarkable fact is that, as Congressional hearings have confirmed, seepage and evaporation at these remote damsites would annually *lose* enough water to supply both Phoenix and Tucson.

As for the remainder, far more efficient power sources are available right now, and at lower net cost. For the truth is, that the Grand Canyon dams will cost far more than they can earn.

6. Recognizing the threat to Grand Canyon, the Bureau of the Budget (which speaks for the President on such matters) has already suggested a moratorium on one of the dams and proposed a commission consider alternatives.

This suggestion has been steadily resisted by Mr. Aspinall's House Committee, which continues to proceed with H. R. 4671. It has been actively fought by the Bureau of Reclamation.

7. At the same time, interestingly, other Bureaus within Secretary Udall's domain (notably National Parks, Fish and Wildlife, Indian Affairs, Mines, Outdoor Recreation, Geological Survey) have been discouraged from presenting their findings, obtained at public expense. Only the Reclamation Bureau has been heard.

8. Meanwhile, in a matter of days the bill will be on the floor of Congress and—let us make the shocking fact completely clear—it will probably pass.

The only thing that can stop it is your prompt action.

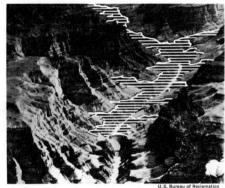

U.S. Bureau of Reclamation

The Grand Canyon: How man plans to improve it. *(Newsweek, May 30, 1966)*

9. What to do? Letters and wires are effective, and so are the forms at right once you have signed them and mailed them. (You will notice that there is also one in the box below to the Sierra Club; that's us.)

10. Remember, with all the complexities of Washington politics and Arizona politics, and the ins and outs of committees and procedures, there is only one simple, incredible issue here: This time it's the Grand Canyon they want to flood. *The Grand Canyon.*

WHAT THE SIERRA CLUB IS FOR

The Sierra Club, founded in 1892 by John Muir, is nonprofit, supported by people who sense what Thoreau sensed when he wrote, "In wildness is the preservation of the world." The club's program is nationwide, includes wilderness trips, books, and films—and a major effort to protect the remnant of wilderness in the Americas.

There are now twenty chapters, branch offices in New York, Washington, Albuquerque, Seattle, and Los Angeles, and a main office in San Francisco.

This advertisement has been made possible by individual contributions, particularly from our Atlantic, Rocky Mountain, Rio Grande, Southern California and Grand Canyon chapter members, and by buyers of Sierra Club books everywhere, especially the twelve in the highly praised Exhibit Format Series, which includes books on Grand Canyon, Glen Canyon, the Redwoods, the Northern Cascades, Mount Everest, and the Sierra.

Sierra Club
Mills Tower
San Francisco, California

☐ Please send me more of the details of the battle to save Grand Canyon.

☐ I know how much this sort of constructive protest costs. Here is my donation of $_____to help you continue your work.

☐ Please send me a copy of "Time and the River Flowing," the famous four-color book by Philip Hyde and François Leydet which tells the whole story of Grand Canyon and the battle to save it. I am enclosing $25.00.

☐ I would like to be a member of the Sierra Club. Enclosed is $14.00 for entrance fee and first year's dues.

Name_____

Address_____

City_____State_____Zip_____

Note: All contributions and membership dues are deductible.

PLEASE CLIP THESE AND MAIL THEM

No. 1

THE PRESIDENT
THE WHITE HOUSE
WASHINGTON 25, D.C.

THANK YOU FOR YOUR STAND, THROUGH THE BUREAU OF THE BUDGET, PROTECTING GRAND CANYON. WOULD YOU PLEASE ASK CONGRESS TO DEFER BOTH GRAND CANYON DAMS PENDING INVESTIGATION OF THE ALTERNATE POWER SOURCES. THANK YOU AGAIN.

Name_____
Address_____
City_____State_____Zip_____

No. 2

SECRETARY OF THE INTERIOR STEWART UDALL
WASHINGTON 25, D.C.

ALL YOUR SPLENDID CONSERVATION WORK OF THE PAST WILL BE BLIGHTED IF YOU ALLOW THE LIVING GRAND CANYON TO DIE AT THE HANDS OF YOUR BUREAU OF RECLAMATION. WOULD YOU PLEASE ALLOW THE FINDINGS OF YOUR OTHER BUREAUS TO BE REPORTED FULLY TO CONGRESS BEFORE THE VOTE ON H.R. 4671? THANK YOU.

Name_____
Address_____
City_____State_____Zip_____

No. 3

REPRESENTATIVE WAYNE ASPINALL
HOUSE OF REPRESENTATIVES
WASHINGTON 25, D.C.

I URGE YOU TO HALT PROCEEDINGS ON H.R. 4671, NOW IN YOUR COMMITTEE, AND TO SEEK EXPERT TESTIMONY FROM THE MANY INTERIOR DEPARTMENT AGENCIES THAT HAVE NOT YET APPEARED BEFORE YOU. THANK YOU.

Name_____
Address_____
City_____State_____Zip_____

No. 4 (To your Congressman)

REPRESENTATIVE _____
HOUSE OF REPRESENTATIVES
WASHINGTON 25, D.C.

PLEASE JOIN IN THE FIGHT TO SAVE GRAND CANYON BY URGING DELETION OF BOTH DAMS PROPOSED IN H.R. 4671. THANK YOU.

Name_____
Address_____
City_____State_____Zip_____

No. 5 (To one of your U.S. Senators)

SENATOR _____
UNITED STATES SENATE
WASHINGTON 25, D.C.

PLEASE JOIN IN THE FIGHT TO SAVE GRAND CANYON BY URGING DELETION OF BOTH DAMS PROPOSED IN H.R. 4671. THANK YOU.

Name_____
Address_____
City_____State_____Zip_____

No. 6 (To your state's other Senator)

SENATOR _____
UNITED STATES SENATE
WASHINGTON 25, D.C.

PLEASE JOIN IN THE FIGHT TO SAVE GRAND CANYON BY URGING DELETION OF BOTH DAMS PROPOSED IN H.R. 4671. THANK YOU.

Name_____
Address_____
City_____State_____Zip_____

Plate 90

space, and chose to run the ad as a full page in the two newspapers—the only two newspapers—that can ever influence legislation in this country: *The New York Times* and the *Washington Post*. Both are read by almost every legislator and Administration official in Washington; and they have in addition a total readership of more than a million educated people in both cities. On June 9 the ad appeared *(Plate 90)*.

Response to the advertisement was astounding. Within a week the club had received more than three thousand membership applications, at $14 each, adding up to almost $50,000 in income. The coupon addressed to Secretary of the Interior Udall was sent in by enough people to require the printing of a form letter in reply. Some congressmen reported that their mail ran in greater volume on this issue—in all of 1966—than on Vietnam, which is an interesting, if confusing, comment on the state of the country.

There was another reaction, one that was not at all what anyone on either side of the issue had expected: by noon of the day the ad appeared, Commissioner of Internal Revenue Sheldon S. Cohen had ordered his San Francisco office to investigate the tax-exempt status of the Sierra Club, and within twenty-four hours he issued a press release addressed to potential members and contributors to the club that he was considering revoking both its tax-exempt status and the tax-deductibility of their future contributions. This, he said, was because the club was engaging in "substantial" political activity, which tax-exempt organizations are not supposed to do, and, until he had made a final determination, he wanted no one to be "taken in" by the club. His action was noted with some interest because it was the first time in history that the Internal Revenue Service had taken such a step.

Cohen, who was said by some Washington observers to have graduated with honors from the LBJ School of Sycophancy, had managed the previous year to stand mute while the American Medical Association spent $1,100,000 of tax-exempt money trying to defeat Medicare. Moreover, he was currently ignoring a tax-exempt $74,000 campaign by an organization called the Central Arizona Project Association, whose sole purpose—as the *Washington Post* pointed out—was to get Congress to enact what the Sierra Club was trying to prevent: the construction of dams in the Grand Canyon. His action against the Sierra Club, therefore, was widely questioned by those curious to learn his criteria. "There are different ways to lobby," he said. "This was so open, so crass, that we had to take notice."[1]

Cohen expected the club to back down, but he grossly underestimated

---

[1]It is accepted in Washington that Cohen was ordered by President Johnson to take the action. It would have been impossible—politically and psychologically—for Cohen to have done it on his own.

SHOULD WE ALSO FLOOD THE SISTINE CHAPEL SO TOURISTS CAN GET NEARER THE CEILING?

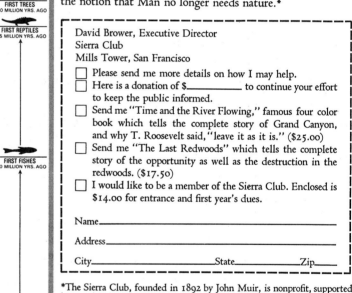

EARTH began four billion years ago and Man two million. The Age of Technology, on the other hand, is hardly a hundred years old, and on our time chart we have been generous to give it even the little line we have.

It seems to us hasty, therefore, during this blip of time, for Man to think of directing his fascinating new tools toward altering irrevocably the forces which made him. Nonetheless, in these few brief years among four billion, wilderness has all but disappeared. And now these:

1) There are proposals *still* before Congress to "improve" Grand Canyon. If they succeed, two dams could back up artificial lakes into 93 miles of canyon gorge. This would benefit tourists in power boats, it is argued, who would enjoy viewing the canyon wall more closely. (See headline.) Submerged underneath the tourists would be part of the most revealing single page of earth's history. The lakes would be as deep as 600 feet (deeper for example, than all but a handful of New York buildings are high) but in a century, silting would have replaced the water with that much mud, wall to wall.

There is no part of the wild Colorado River, the Grand Canyon's sculptor, that would not be maimed.

Tourist recreation, as a reason for the dams, is in fact an afterthought. The Bureau of Reclamation, which has backed them, calls the dams "cash registers." It expects they'll make money by sale of commercial power.

They will not provide anyone with water.

2) In Northern California, during only the last 115 years, nearly *all* the private virgin redwood forests have been cut down.

Where nature's tallest living things have stood silently since the age of the dinosaurs, there is, incredibly, argument against a proposed park at Redwood Creek which would save a mere 2% of the virgin growth that was once there. For having cut so much and taken the rest for granted, the lumber companies are eager to get on with business. They see little reason why they should not.

The companies have said tourists want only enough roadside trees for the snapping of photos. They offered to spare trees for this purpose, and not much more. The result would remind you of the places on your face you missed while you were shaving.

3) And up the Hudson, there are plans for a power complex —a plant, transmission lines, and a reservoir near and on Storm King Mountain—effectively destroying one of the last wild and high and beautiful spots near New York City.

4) A proposal to flood a region in Alaska as large as Lake Erie would eliminate at once the breeding grounds of more wildlife than conservationists have preserved in history.

5) In San Francisco, real estate interests have for years been filling a bay that made the city famous, putting tract houses over the fill; and now there's a new idea—still more fill, enough for an air cargo terminal as big as Manhattan.

There exists today a mentality which can conceive such destruction, giving commerce as ample reason. For 74 years, the Sierra Club (now with 48,000 members) has opposed that mentality. But now, when even Grand Canyon is endangered, we are at a critical moment in time.

This generation will decide if something untrammelled and free remains, as testimony we had love for those who follow.

We have been taking ads, therefore, asking people to write their Congressmen and Senators; Secretary of the Interior Stewart Udall; The President; and to send us funds to continue the battle. Thousands *have* written, but meanwhile, Grand Canyon legislation *still* stands a chance of passage. More letters are needed and much more money, to help fight the notion that Man no longer needs nature.*

David Brower, Executive Director
Sierra Club
Mills Tower, San Francisco

☐ Please send me more details on how I may help.
☐ Here is a donation of $_____ to continue your effort to keep the public informed.
☐ Send me "Time and the River Flowing," famous four color book which tells the complete story of Grand Canyon, and why T. Roosevelt said, "leave it as it is." ($25.00)
☐ Send me "The Last Redwoods" which tells the complete story of the opportunity as well as the destruction in the redwoods. ($17.50)
☐ I would like to be a member of the Sierra Club. Enclosed is $14.00 for entrance and first year's dues.

Name_____

Address_____

City_____State_____Zip_____

---

*The Sierra Club, founded in 1892 by John Muir, is nonprofit, supported by people who, like Thoreau, believe "In wildness is the preservation of the world." The club's program is nationwide, includes wilderness trips, books and films—as well as such efforts as this to protect the remnant of wilderness in the Americas. There are now twenty chapters, branch offices in New York (Biltmore Hotel), Washington (Dupont Circle Building), Los Angeles (Auditorium Building), Albuquerque, Seattle, and main office in San Francisco.

(Our previous ads, urging that readers exercise a constitutional right of petition to save Grand Canyon from two dams which would have flooded it, produced an unprecedented reaction by the Internal Revenue Service threatening our tax deductible status. IRS called the ads a "substantial" effort to "influence legislation." Undefined, these terms leave organizations like ours at the mercy of administrative whim. [The question has not been raised with organizations that favor Grand Canyon dams.] So we cannot now promise that contributions you send us are deductible — pending result of what may be a long legal battle.)

Plate 91

Dinosaur and Big Bend. Glacier and Grand Teton, Kings Canyon, Redwoods, Mammoth, Even Yellowstone and Yosemite. And The Wild Rivers, and Wilderness.

How Can You Guarantee These, Mr. Udall, If Grand Canyon Is Dammed For Profit?

1) A bill will soon be voted in Congress (H.R. 4671) which would put two dams into Grand Canyon, maiming for all time the wild river that has been the canyon's sculptor for 25,000,000 years.

2) If the bill passes, two artificial lakes will back up into 133 miles of canyon gorge. And hardly a century later, silting will have created wall to wall mud and tangled growth.

3) In some places, the inner gorge will be submerged five hundred feet. A vital part of "The most revealing single page of the earth's history," as Joseph Wood Krutch has described it, will be drowned.

4) It is argued that artificial lakes will be an "improvement" because tourists will be nearer the walls.

Should we flood the Sistine Chapel, so tourists can float nearer the ceiling?

5) Between the lakes, the Colorado's depth will vary fifteen feet from day to day, depending on hydroelectric demand.

Shoreline campsites will become suddenly dangerous. Wildlife will be disrupted, as will the ecology of one of history's treasures.

There is no part of the Colorado River within Grand Canyon that would not be affected.

6) The dams will not be used for water. They are called "cash registers" by the Bureau of Reclamation. They are expected to make money by sale of commercial power.

7) But for even the making of money, Grand Canyon dams will soon be as obsolete as they are unnecessary. Congressional testimony established they are fantastically expensive and wasteful of water. Still the alternatives are ignored.

8) The real push for the dams is political—an attempt by the seven states in the Colorado Basin to finance diversion of water from the Columbia River to the Colorado, at a cost of an undetermined number of billions of dollars to the other states.

9) If the bill does pass, no national park will be safe. With the unthinkable precedent set in Grand Canyon, it will be simple to approve dams or other commercial projects *already proposed* in a dozen national parks.

10) If the bill passes, America will have violated a treaty obligation signed at the International Convention on Nature Protection and Wildlife Preservation, that it would never subject a national park to exploitation for commercial profit.

Our entire National Park System, so brilliant it has been a model for every nation in the world, would suddenly be meaningless.

11) Secretary of the Interior Stewart Udall could do much to save the day.

Taking advantage of the important new evidence presented in the House hearings, he could urge the dams be deleted from H.R. 4671. He could urge that Congressional committees at least hear the findings of his National Park Service, Bureaus of Récreation, and Mines and Geological Survey, instead of only Reclamation.

By failure to act, Mr. Udall is assisting the demise of the great park system he was pledged to protect.

12) It is an accident of history, but it is this generation which must assure that something untrammeled and free remains in the American earth as testimony that we had love for the people who follow.

13) It is for all the above reasons that we ran the two advertisements on June 9th— protesting the destruction of Grand Canyon —that produced an unprecedented reaction by the Internal Revenue Service.

By 4 P.M. the next day, an IRS messenger delivered a letter to us in San Francisco. It cast a cloud over our tax deductible status, effectively stopping major financial assistance for our public service program.

IRS read the ads as a sudden attempt to "influence legislation" in a "substantial" way. (They do not define those terms, leaving organizations like ours at the mercy of administrative whim.) *And they do not even raise the question with organizations that favor the dams.*

270 FT.

Vasey's Paradise at Marble Gorge, where a fantastic natural spring gushes out of the sheer rock canyon wall, will be submerged by 270 feet of water. The Statue of Liberty and its base, placed at this spot, would have only its upper arm and torch showing above the water. If the dams are built in Grand Canyon, 133 miles of inner gorge will be submerged by water as deep as *500 feet*, and later by that much mud.

14) The Sierra Club has been in the business of helping people enjoy and save natural beauty for 74 years. Nothing new has been added to this goal in that time, except that the battle to save Grand Canyon is now in its critical phase.

If the IRS succeeds in slowing us down, it will also have slowed every organization which chooses to work for the saving of our resources. And this is no time to slow down.

15) Therefore, tax deductible or not, we intend to continue. After all, as astonishing as it may seem, it *is* the Grand Canyon that's in danger this time. *The Grand Canyon.*

16) Possibly within the next two weeks, the House Committee on Interior and Insular Affairs will have reported out the bill and it will be ready for a floor vote in the House.

You can stop it by adding your coupons to those that have been sent already, or better still, your own letters.

And while we cannot now promise that any contributions you send us are deductible, a determination still in the hands of IRS, we *can* promise the funds will help fight the remaining battles against a technology that feels it no longer needs nature.

WHAT THE SIERRA CLUB IS FOR

The Sierra Club, founded in 1892 by John Muir, is nonprofit, supported by people who sense what Thoreau sensed when he wrote, "In wildness is the preservation of the world." The club's program is nationwide, includes wilderness trips, books, and films —and a major effort to protect the remnant of wilderness in the Americas.

There are now twenty chapters, branch offices in New York, Washington, Albuquerque, Seattle, and Los Angeles, and a main office in San Francisco.

This advertisement has been made possible by individual contributions, particularly from our Atlantic, Rocky Mountain, Rio Grande, Southern California and Grand Canyon chapter members, and by buyers of Sierra Club books everywhere, especially the twelve in the highly praised Exhibit Format Series, which includes books on Grand Canyon, Glen Canyon, the Redwoods, the Northern Cascades, Mount Everest, and the Sierra.

Plate 92

Brower, who now called his own press conference to say that he was fighting the IRS action. ("I might point out," said Cohen later, rather petulantly, "that the Sierra Club immediately turned to the news media, before any effort to present its case to the Service." Since the IRS had been the first to publicize its action, however, it is hard to know what else he thought the club should have done.) But Cohen, who insisted that he had never heard of the Sierra Club prior to June 9, stuck to his guns in spite of such setbacks as receiving a well-publicized open letter from twelve congressmen informing him that they each were making $10 contributions to the Sierra Club and claiming them as deductions on their 1966 tax returns.

The two dams had been budgeted at a cost of more than $1 billion, and were to be built by the Interior Department's Bureau of Reclamation (the bureau's slogan is "We like to push rivers around," which drives Brower up the wall). Because of this, many people thought that Cohen had been put up to his action by Secretary Udall, since Udall's brother was the congressman behind the project. But, though he was too weak politically to veto the dams, Stewart had never been in favor of the project. He said later that he first learned of the IRS action from his news ticker, and that his first thought was that the Sierra Club had contrived the action to win public sympathy.

Udall was right in guessing that the IRS action would win the club a good deal of public sympathy. In fact, it won them much more than that. Cohen had cut off the club from about $100,000 in contributions it might otherwise have gotten, but the advertising campaign brought in more than $225,000 in new gifts and memberships. In the year beginning that June, the club acquired more than fifteen thousand new members, bringing total membership to more than fifty thousand. But Udall, and Cohen, had missed the far more important point that the ad itself was making. It was saying, in effect, "Can you believe it? The government is actually going to dam up the Grand Canyon! Really and truly, the Grand Canyon!"

In July, a few weeks after the first ad, Mander wrote one of the most eloquent ads ever to appear in this country *(Plate 91)*. The ad was placed in a small list of intellectual magazines ranging from *The National Review* on the right to *Ramparts* on the left. It later was reprinted—free, and at the request of the publishers—in *Scientific American* and other magazines, and in about a dozen newspapers across the country.

Two weeks later, he ran a third ad, this time in *The New York Times* alone *(Plate 92)*. By this time there was enough money to repeat the first ad in additional newspapers around the country, and with that repeat the campaign was essentially over. The three ads cost a total of $50,000 in media and production charges. What did they accomplish?

The project bill was killed in the House of Representatives on the motion of the committee chairman who had backed it all along. He decided not to allow the House even to vote on it. In the Senate, a vote was finally taken in the spring of 1967, and the measure, which had passed in 1966, was defeated by a vote of 70 to 12, one of the most dramatic reversals on a major issue in Senate history. "It was like fighting dinosaurs," Gossage later commented. "They couldn't even conceive of how to fight us."

Mander said later, "I doubt we'd have gotten the response we have had if the damming of the Grand Canyon was the first technological encroachment of our time. The critical point is that even those who aren't in love with the place as a *sight* care a hell of a lot about the kind of mind that would casually sacrifice it. It's the *mentality* that's the real danger, not so much the filling-in or destruction of any single resource. It's the mentality that is capable of ignoring ecology, and its relation to all of life, and of ignoring man's need for, and pleasure in, some reminders—even in urban situations —that we are not machinery; that we have something to do with the natural world."

The Last Cigarette Campaign

People who devote a lot of time to being on the "right" side of moral issues, like the Sierra Club or anti-militarist groups, are accustomed to fighting a series of strategic retreats; at each stage, one extracts as many concessions from the enemy as possible, then withdraws, regroups, and tries to meet the next assault, whether on a physical environment or a population. The only action is a counterattack, the only victory a stalemate.

But for the last cigarette campaign, however, the situation was completely reversed. At its start, cigarettes were sold freely across the United States; more than half of all adults smoked; most of those were physically addicted and would find it very hard to quit; the cigarette business was extremely profitable to everyone from tobacco farmers (the Department of Agriculture supported the price) and manufacturers to advertising agencies and media ($250 million spent on advertising in 1969), and of course provided federal, state and local governments with billions of dollars each year in taxes. The only opponents of cigarettes were some do-gooders who wanted to save people from their own willful acts, hardly a guarantee of success.

And yet that was the interesting thing about the whole antismoking campaign, which is, of course, what the last cigarette campaign was.

Plate 93

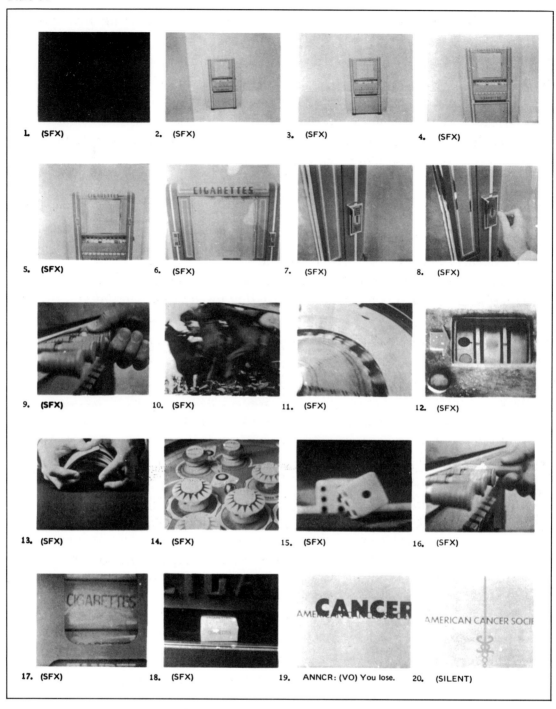

1. (SFX) 2. (SFX) 3. (SFX) 4. (SFX)
5. (SFX) 6. (SFX) 7. (SFX) 8. (SFX)
9. (SFX) 10. (SFX) 11. (SFX) 12. (SFX)
13. (SFX) 14. (SFX) 15. (SFX) 16. (SFX)
17. (SFX) 18. (SFX) 19. ANNCR: (VO) You lose. 20. (SILENT)

Those who were involved in it had absolutely no ulterior motive. They
could not make a penny from it, they would never be invited to sit in on
the *Tonight* show, they had no substitute product to sell; and if they
became too well known as personalities, their professional reputations
would come under suspicion. Nevertheless, a small group of devoted
people, working largely independently of each other, managed in five
years to bring a $2 billion industry to its knees; to a point, in fact, where

in June of 1969 it begged the favor of being allowed to cease its broadcast advertising over a period of a year rather than six months.

Not everyone would agree, of course, that the industry was groveling for small favors. Donald S. Hillman, director of television, films and radio for the American Cancer Society, said in mid-1969: "Let me tell you quite frankly that the cigarette companies would dearly love to pull out of advertising. The $250 million they spend each year could go into dividends to the stockholders, raising the price of the stocks; it could go into diversification [the tobacco companies have been buying into the food and beverage business, and the American Tobacco Company changed its name in 1969 to American Products, Inc.]; and I don't think their total sales would be hurt too much."

To which Congressman John Moss of California, a leader in the fight against cigarettes, replied: "If they would so dearly love to, I don't see anyone holding them back. Since the first congressional moves against cigarettes in 1965, they have had four more years in which to promote their product and claim new addicts, who will be their customers for the major part of their lives."

But even Moss would agree that it is only a matter of time before all promotion of cigarettes is ended. Television advertising came toward its end when all three networks agreed to refuse it after September 30, 1970. Other media have seldom been effective for tobacco companies, and are likely to be dropped within a few years. If the companies should resort to the direct-mail, free-sample technique of many package-goods manufacturers, they would probably be taking their lives in their hands in terms of the response from nonsmokers. The interesting question is discovering how all this came about.

With regard to the antismoking advertising campaign itself, most of the work was done by the American Cancer Society. The ACS did its first research in the late 1940s, when it noticed a statistical correlation between the incidence of lung cancer and whether the victim was or was not a cigarette smoker. It commissioned a statistical study of 187,000 men between the ages of fifty and sixty, taking medical and biographical information from them, including everything possible about their smoking habits. The men were followed for three years, and, for those who died in that period, every effort was made to learn the cause of death—from autopsies, death certificates, or attending doctors. The study confirmed that heavy smokers were much more likely to die of lung cancer than men who smoked little, and that these, in turn, were more likely to die of lung cancer than were nonsmokers. This was the study on which the *Reader's Digest* based much of its famous report in 1958.

Although the findings have been amplified and refined a great deal since then, as the relationship of cigarette smoking to other causes of death became known, the essential facts are as follows:

Of every 1,000 men between twenty-five and sixty-five who are nonsmokers: 223 will have died by their sixty-fifth birthday.

Of every 1,000 men between twenty-five and sixty-five who smoke one pack a day: 387 will have died by their sixty-fifth birthday.

Of every 1,000 men between twenty-five and sixty-five who smoke

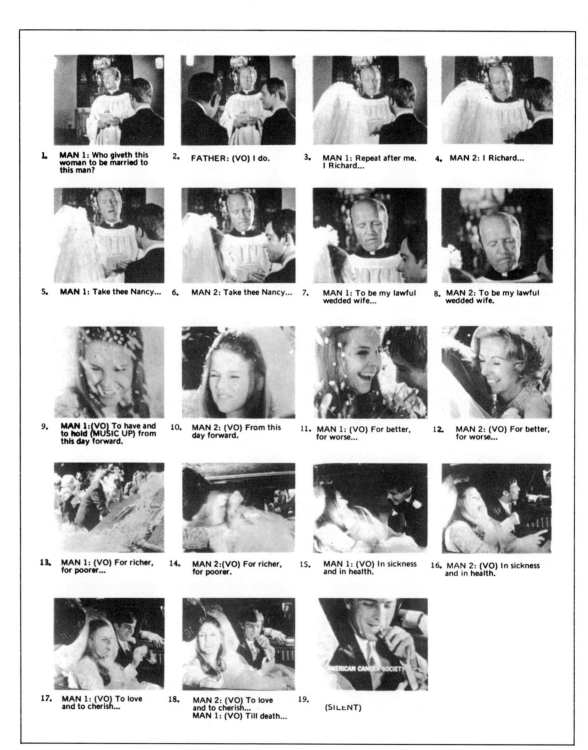

Plate 94

Plate 95

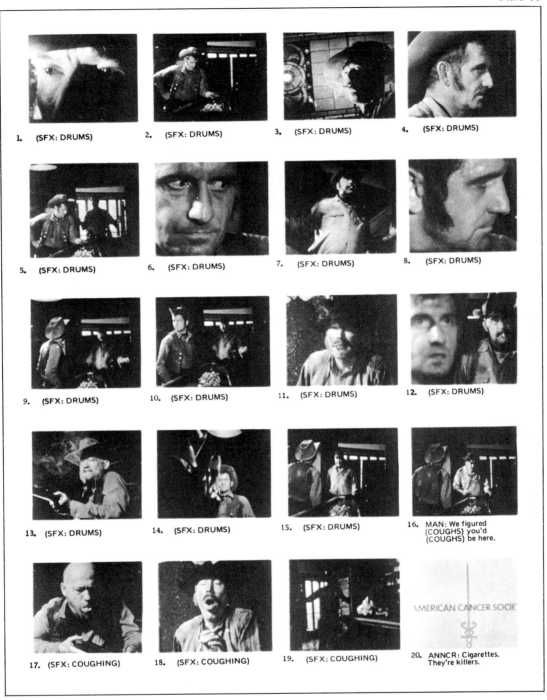

1. (SFX: DRUMS)
2. (SFX: DRUMS)
3. (SFX: DRUMS)
4. (SFX: DRUMS)
5. (SFX: DRUMS)
6. (SFX: DRUMS)
7. (SFX: DRUMS)
8. (SFX: DRUMS)
9. (SFX: DRUMS)
10. (SFX: DRUMS)
11. (SFX: DRUMS)
12. (SFX: DRUMS)
13. (SFX: DRUMS)
14. (SFX: DRUMS)
15. (SFX: DRUMS)
16. MAN: We figured (COUGHS) you'd (COUGHS) be here.
17. (SFX: COUGHING)
18. (SFX: COUGHING)
19. (SFX: COUGHING)
20. ANNCR: Cigarettes. They're killers.

two packs a day: 460 will have died by their sixty-fifth birthday.

In 1960 the society wrote and produced its first television commercial (it does not have an advertising agency). It showed Bob Cousy reading, in a sincere, amateurish way, a little homily on developing good habits for sports, like not smoking. It made the spot available to its chapters around the country, and asked them to place it on local television stations as a public service message, while the New York headquarters tried to place it with the networks. The society was dismayed to learn that most stations would not run the commercial because it offended the cigarette companies, who were among their largest advertisers.

Shocked by its discovery of the facts of advertising life, the society petitioned the Federal Communications Commission to require that stations carry the spot. But in the absence of official government statistics, the FCC refused to touch the problem. There was no evidence, they said, showing a causal relationship between cigarette smoking and these diseases, and until there was, they weren't going to do a thing. The society, along with the American Heart Association, the Tuberculosis and Respiratory Diseases Association and the Public Health Service then petitioned President Kennedy, requesting him to commission a study of the problem. He did, and the result was the 1964 report of the Surgeon-General. Armed with this, the society, as the major advertiser among the anticigarette groups, went back to the FCC to plead its case.

But the news had already reached the FCC, where the antismoking forces had an ally in Henry Geller, general counsel to the commission, who as early as 1961 had been confronted with evidence in the matter ("A man named Sidney Katz, whose wife had died of lung cancer, came to me and asked why these things could be advertised. . . "). After the release of the Surgeon-General's report, Geller decided that the next complaint he got from the antismoking people would become his test case and would be brought up to the seven FCC commissioners for a ruling on the fairness of denying them air time.

In February, 1966, he got that complaint: a letter from a lawyer named John Banzhaf, which served as the basis of his case. Knowing his commissioners—five of the seven were laughable hacks in the hip pocket of the broadcast station owners—he persuaded them to discuss the matter quickly and in total secrecy, before the broadcasters could get to them. There is some evidence that had the commissioners known the furor their decision would create, they might have decided the other way. At any rate, by mid-May the commission ruled unanimously that it was a violation of the so-called fairness doctrine for a station to deny time to antismoking commercials, and the way was opened for the society and others to speak frankly about smoking (Plates 93–95).

Perhaps the most famous spot was made by William Talman, six weeks before he died. He was the actor who played the district attorney on the *Perry Mason* television series, the perennial foil for Raymond Burr. Talman had been a heavy smoker all his life, and—in the summer of 1968—was dying of lung cancer. A story appeared in *Variety* that the society was having trouble getting actors to appear in its commercials, because they were afraid of losing work from cigarette companies. Talman had his wife call Hillman at the society, and volunteered to make a

Plate 96

AMERICAN CANCER SOCIETY

SCENES OF TALMAN FAMILY
IN VARIOUS PHASES OF
ACTIVITY AROUND THE HOME.

This is the house we live in. That's
Billy, he's pretty handy to have around;
Steve, home from college; Barbie, looking
after her brother Timmy; Debbie, who'll
soon graduate from high school; Susan,
who has captured all our hearts; and my
wife Peggy, who looks after all of us.

CLOSEUP OF PHOTOGRAPH
WITH TALMAN AND RAYMOND
BURR.

And that's me - Bill Talman, with a friend
of mine you might recognize. He used to
beat my brains out on TV every week for
about ten years.

MEDIUM CLOSEUP OF TALMAN
IN DEN.

You know, I didn't really mind losing
those courtroom battles. But I'm in a
battle right now I don't want to lose at
all because, if I lose it, it means losing
my wife and those kids you just met.

CLOSEUP OF BILL TALMAN.

I've got lung cancer.
So take some advice about smoking and
losing from someone whose been doing both
for years. If you haven't smoked, don't
start. If you do smoke, quit. Don't be
a loser.

AMERICAN CANCER SOCIETY
LOGOTYPE BOTTOM SUPERIM-
POSED OVER TALMAN.

personal commercial. A film crew was flown out to Hollywood the next day, and Talman, though obviously at the end of his strength, narrated it as a personal testimonial *(Plate 96)*.

Even without the network agreement of 1969, and the subsequently enacted federal law of 1970 prohibiting broadcast cigarette advertising after January 1, 1971, it is likely that the American Cancer Society commercials, together with those of the American Heart Association and the Tuberculosis and Respiratory Diseases Association, would have driven cigarettes off the air in a few years. This is because the "fairness doctrine" says that the more times cigarette commercials are played, the more times anticigarette commercials must be played to keep on a parity with them. No one likes to spend money, particularly on the order of $250 million a year, advertising something that is required by law to draw its own attack fifteen minutes after it appears.

It might be instructive to close with a comparison of the costs—for both sides—of the advertising fight. In the five years 1965–1969, cigarette manufacturers spent just over $1 billion to advertise their product. This does not include the cost of public relations, or of the Tobacco Research Institute, financed by the manufacturers to find evidence that might contradict the findings of the Surgeon-General's report (it has not, to date, found any).

In the same five years, the total cost to the American Cancer Society of producing all advertising and promotional material relating to cigarette smoking (the society does not have to pay for air time, since it is a public service organization) was just under $2 million—evidently just the right amount to win the fight.

Postscript

Sometimes even the most successful advertising campaigns have unexpected results. David Ogilvy's "At 60 miles per hour . . . " for Rolls-Royce almost bankrupted the client, and cost him the account. Foote, Cone & Belding's Contac campaign got so expensive that the agency was fired, even though sales were extremely good. And two years after the Grand Canyon campaign, David Brower was fired from his job as Executive Director of the Sierra Club for being too much of an activist. Many people in the advertising business wonder if it really matters anyway.

And sometimes they have a point. A good deal of so-called "public service" advertising is so tied to outdated values as to defeat its own purpose. The Urban Coalition's "Give a damn," for example, is middle-class Christmas basketing of the worst sort, for as long as whites have someone to "give a damn" about—their little black brothers, in this case—they can have their egos massaged at little cost to themselves. And what is one to make of the Advertising Council's campaign asking for donations to Radio Free Europe—two years after its exposure as an arm of the CIA?

But maybe it *does* matter. It was the Grand Canyon campaign, after all, that started the whole ecology boom. When Mander, Brower and Gossage saved Grand Canyon with three ads and a budget of $50,000, they tapped an activist vein in Americans that had never before been touched. With those ads, they beat both Congress and the Johnson Administration, succeeding where everyone else—*everyone else*—had failed. Tens of thousands of previously uninterested people joined the Sierra Club because of the ads, and those thousands were followed by millions more who were finally becoming concerned about stopping the rape of the planet. Brower went on to form the Friends of the Earth, an activist organization whose purpose is to work politically for conservation of the environment, and Mander is on his board of directors.

It's a good sign.